BREAD

······

MACHINE
MAGIC

BREAD

MACHINE
MAGIC

139 EXCITING NEW RECIPES CREATED
ESPECIALLY FOR USE IN ALL TYPES OF
BREAD MACHINES

LINDA REHBERG
LOIS CONWAY

ILLUSTRATIONS BY LOIS SIMMONS

ST. MARTIN'S PRESS
NEW YORK

To our mothers, Estelle and Dulcinea, who were with us in spirit every step of the way.

◆◆◆◆◆◆◆◆◆◆◆

BREAD MACHINE MAGIC. Copyright © 1992 by Linda Rehberg and Lois Conway. Illustrations copyright © 1992 by Lois Simmons. All rights reserved. Printed in the United States of America. No part of this book may be used or reproduced in any manner whatsoever without written permission except in the case of brief quotations embodied in critical articles or reviews. For information, address St. Martin's Press, 175 Fifth Avenue, New York, N.Y. 10010.

Designed by SNAP • HAUS GRAPHICS, Diane Stevenson
Library of Congress Cataloging-in-Publication Data

Rehberg, Linda.
    Bread machine magic / Linda Rehberg and Lois Conway.
        p.   cm.
    ISBN 0-312-06914-6 (paperback original)
    1. Bread. I. Conway, Lois. II. Title.
TX769.R38 1992
641.8′15—dc20   91-41596
                           CIP

25 24 23 22 21 20 19 18

•• CONTENTS ••

✸✸ ACKNOWLEDGMENTS ✸✸

This book could not have been written without the assistance of Cheri Cotton Ginsberg, our associate baker and taster. She's allergic to yeast so her efforts went far beyond what was asked of her. Cheri, you are incredible!

Putting our ideas on paper was made possible through the computer knowledge and invaluable assistance of Debbie and Rick Carlson. It was such a relief knowing you were only a phone call away! Mega-thanks to you both.

We are indebted to family members who offered their support and many good friends who tasted and critiqued each loaf we made, often several times over until we got it right! Thank you Madelyn and Bob Robenhymer, Gary and Rita Gottshalk, Dave and Terri Browne, Sue and Steve Garfin, Gil and Carolyn Andrade, DeDe and Shareen Carlson, Susan Schelkun, Bill and Elise Mungovan, Elliot and Sara, Michael, Eric and Janey, Anita, Morris and Evelyn Schaffran, the wonderfully supportive ladies from the North Clairemont Library, the great cooks and connoisseurs of the Wrangler Square Dance Club, the fantastic faculty and staff of Poway High School, the ever-hungry "Cosmo Club" regulars, the hard-working real estate agents in the Clairemont Coldwell Banker office, co-workers at Smokenders who had to put up with our incessant bread discussions, and our favorite tester, Briscoe, the soft-coated wheaten terrier. We're grateful to Lou Ramsey, Max Hagan, and Janet Swanson for their special contributions to this book. By the way, Lynn Dominguez, you started it all! Most of all we wish to thank some very special friends: Margaret Smith, Lorraine Flora, Irene Billingsley—a team of co-workers that makes each workday a delight. Your enthusiastic support, highly valued opinions, and marvelous senses of humor were an integral part of this project. Our heartfelt appreciation to Marilyn Lauer who cheered us on from the sidelines. Now that this book is done, Marilyn, we hope you'll bake more than one type of bread in your machine!

Shayna (our "in-house editor"), you were a great help. Even though you're so much smarter than your mom, your gentle spirit prevented you from flaunting it. Thanks, "kiddo."

We wish to acknowledge Dr. Nancy Gamble and Lucy Silvay Peluso, both authors, psychologists, and friends who set an inspiring example with their own successes.

We extend additional expressions of gratitude to two men who helped us through the transition from wishful thinking to reality: Lloyd Billingsley, who gave us sound advice and guidance and a glimpse of the dedication it takes to write full time; and Frank Phillips, a legal consultant extraordinaire—there should be more attorneys like him!

Bread Machine Magic would not be a reality without our editor, Barbara Anderson. Her warmth, wit, and superb editing skills contributed greatly to the fulfillment of our dream.

Our husbands, Dennis and Jim, deserve applause. They never flinched as we brought home one bread machine after another. They endured inaccessible phone lines and computers, numerous "courier" runs on their way home from work, nonexistent wives at several social events, and freezers crammed full of frozen breads and rolls instead of their marinated steaks. Pack up the RVs, guys; the book is finally done and it's time to go play!

INTRODUCTION

Welcome to the world of bread baking made easy! With an automatic bread machine and five minutes of your time, you can create an almost endless variety of delicious, healthful loaves to please your family or shower on friends. Gone are the rolled-up sleeves, floured hands, and aching muscles from trying to stir that last cup of flour into an unyielding dough. Kneading and punching the dough may have been good "therapy" years ago; it's aerobics and weight training these days. The four or five hours once spent tending a rising loaf of bread can now be programmed into the bread machine to suit our busy schedules. The nicest bonus of all is waking up any given morning to the delectable, heady aroma of freshly baked bread! How can any day go wrong when it starts like that?

Because freshly baked homemade bread has such a wonderful taste and texture, it's the perfect gift when you want to say a simple thank-you or when you're invited for dinner and don't know what to bring. It's a gift that's always appreciated. We know a real estate agent who bakes a loaf whenever she meets clients for a listing. It's also a delightful way to greet new neighbors. When you have company over, the bread machine creates a special perfume of its own. Nothing says "welcome" faster than the smell of baking bread.

You probably already own a bread machine and are well aware of its many advantages. But, chances are, you picked up this book for the very same reason we were motivated to write it. For all their advantages, most machines come with just a few rather uninspired recipes. That's a major disappointment for those of us who have grand visions of creating an endless variety of healthful whole-grain breads, unusual fruit and vegetable breads, delicious white breads for sandwiches, European ryes and pumpernickels, luscious sweet rolls and coffee cakes—maybe even a sourdough bread if it isn't too complicated.

With those breads in mind, we tossed out the recipe booklets and set out to create our own masterpieces. What we created, however, were a lot of disasters! We'd never seen so many ugly loaves of bread! How discouraging to discover that "blue ribbon" breads aren't easy to produce, at least for a novice.

We retrieved the recipe booklets and started again from scratch, but we had many questions that went beyond the basic instructions in our bread machine booklets. It became necessary to back up and do a great deal of research on bread baking techniques to find the answers. We've compiled much of that knowledge and our experiences in the chapter Tips for Baking the Perfect Loaf.

Once we had answers, our next challenge was to adapt all that we had learned to the unique requirements of each of the leading brands of bread machines. That could only be accomplished by purchasing the machines and testing more than one thousand loaves of bread. Boy, did those machines get a workout! We tested our recipes on the Hitachi and both the large and small Panasonic/National and Welbilt bread machines. We specifically chose the Panasonic/National and the Welbilt machines for testing purposes because the amounts of liquid and yeast required in their recipes vary from all the other machines we've seen on the market. (It's our understanding that the Regal and Sanyo are basically the same machine as the Hitachi, and the Dak is identical to the Welbilt.)

Probably our most difficult task was maintaining our composure when time and again a favorite loaf would turn out beautifully in one machine, but not in the others. Our goal was to produce recipes that made consistently acceptable loaves in all five machines. Rather than sacrifice a good recipe, because one of the five loaves occasionally failed to meet our standards for height or appearance, we made a notation at the beginning of those particular recipes.

As you can imagine, all those loaves of bread needed sampling, too. We enlisted the aid of many valued, opinionated tasters: spouses, children, friends, co-workers, relatives, neighbors, even Lois's dog, Briscoe! Pavlov would have been proud of him. The moment the machine beeped that a loaf was done, Briscoe dashed into the kitchen, screeched to a halt in front of the bread machine, and waited for the first slice, his salivary glands working overtime.

Our cooking backgrounds and food preferences differ dramatically, and this book reflects that broad range of tastes. We both work for Smokenders, although our full-time occupation at the present seems to be bread baking! Lois's forte is gourmet cooking. Easily bored, she prefers concocting new recipes. A good part of her weekend is spent in the kitchen creating unique and lavish meals. To Lois, heaven is sun-dried tomatoes and goat cheese on French bread. Linda, on the other hand, is more the meat-and-potatoes type of cook. She has taught basic cooking skills to both special-education and gifted students. Cooking at home is done on the run and the fewer ingredients, the better. A BLT on toasted sourdough is more her version of nirvana.

We are both convinced that in years to come, the automatic bread machine will be found in most kitchens. It meets two very modern needs: it's an appliance that is quick and easy to use; and it enables us to put healthier whole-grain and preservative-free breads on our tables.

This cookbook contains more than 130 fabulous new recipes for your bread machine. We know many of them will become family favorites that you'll find yourself baking time and again. Though the recipes for dinner rolls, coffee cakes, and specialty breads require more time and effort, we hope you won't overlook them. We believe many of the best recipes in the book are in those chapters. You'll find most of them take less than an additional 30 minutes to create. Even if you don't consider yourself a baker, we urge you to give them a try. If you've never made homemade cinnamon rolls or pita bread, you're in for a real treat!

With *Bread Machine Magic* in hand, we feel you, too, can strike out on your own, adapting and creating just about any bread recipe you desire. In the next chapter, we discuss the basic ingredients and provide more detailed information on the limitations and capabilities of this marvelous new appliance.

We've had great fun concocting recipes for almost every type of bread imaginable—even the failures tasted yummy! Now it's your turn. May your days of bread-machine baking be filled with miracles and magic!

TIPS FOR BAKING THE PERFECT LOAF

INGREDIENTS ◆◆◆◆◆◆◆◆◆◆◆◆◆◆◆◆◆◆◆◆◆◆◆◆◆◆◆◆◆◆◆◆◆

As any good cook or baker will tell you, the secret to success lies in using the best possible ingredients. The same is true for breads. Always try to obtain the most recently milled flours, the freshest vegetables, the ripest fruit, the freshest yeast. You'll notice a difference! Here are some guidelines that should help.

WHITE FLOURS
Bread flour is now sold in most grocery stores. (Gold Medal packages it as "Better for Bread" flour.) It has a higher gluten content than all-purpose flour. Gluten gives structure and height to each loaf, therefore bread flour will produce a higher loaf of bread (also, one with a coarser texture) and should be used in the recipes where it's indicated.

We switch to **all-purpose** (bleached or unbleached) flour for most dinner rolls, sweet rolls, and specialty breads, as well as for loaves that rise too high with bread flour. Both bleached and unbleached all-purpose white flours are refined; however, bleached flour has also been whitened with chlorine. Whether you choose bleached or unbleached flour, any difference in texture, flavor, or height in the finished product is indiscernible.

WHOLE-GRAIN FLOURS
Whole wheat flour, unlike white flour, is ground from the complete wheat berry and thus contains the wheat germ as well as the wheat bran. Avoid using stoneground whole wheat in the bread machine. It is coarser in texture and does not rise as well as regular whole wheat flour.

Rye flour is a heavy flour milled from the rye grain. It is low in gluten. You will need to combine it with white or whole wheat flour to produce an acceptable-size loaf. It also makes a sticky dough.

Barley flour is milled from barley kernels, which are very high in minerals. It contributes a slightly sweet taste and a cakelike texture to the dough.

Buckwheat flour has a strong, tart, and earthy flavor and lends a grayish color to the finished product. We use it in small quantities because a little goes a long way.

Millet flour is ground from whole millet and when added to bread, gives it a crumbly, dry taste and texture.

Oats have the highest protein and mineral content of all grains. They add that sweet and nutty "country" richness to bread.

Cracked wheat and **bulgur** are pieces of the wheat kernel. Bulgur is cracked wheat that has been parboiled and dried for faster cooking. It will absorb liquids more readily than cracked wheat.

Bran is the outer covering of the wheat kernel. It is added to bread recipes for texture, flavor, and fiber. Use it sparingly since too much bran (more than ⅓ cup in the 1-pound loaf or ½ cup in the 1½-pound loaf) can inhibit the yeast's growth. Most supermarkets now carry miller's bran in a box. Check the cereal or health-food section of your market.

Wheat germ is the tiny embryo of the wheat kernel. It contributes texture and a nutty flavor to whole-grain breads. If used in excess (more than ¼ cup per loaf), it will inhibit the rising action of the yeast. Sold normally in jars, you will probably locate it in the cereal or health-food section of your grocery store.

Millet is a yellowish, round grain that resembles a mustard seed. It adds a crunchy texture and extra nutrition to your breads.

We had no difficulty locating the various whole grains used in these recipes at local natural-foods stores. The larger stores offer them both packaged and in open bins. Compare prices and we think you'll discover that buying them in bulk from the bins is a better deal.

Whole-grain breads do not rise as quickly as white-flour breads and are normally shorter, denser loaves when made in a bread machine. (The newer machines, however, take that fact into account and allow a longer rising period when baking whole-grain breads.) Only wheat and rye flours contain gluten; therefore, all whole-grain recipes require white and/or whole wheat flour as a base.

Whole-grain breads also brown faster and have a more robust flavor. We often used the Light Crust setting for the whole-grain breads to avoid over-browning.

It's important to note that whole-grain flours and wheat germ contain natural oils and will soon go rancid if stored at room temperature. We store them in airtight containers in the freezer.

LIQUIDS

THE WELBILT AND DAK BREAD MACHINES USUALLY REQUIRE IN-CREASED AMOUNTS OF LIQUID TO CREATE A SOFTER DOUGH FOR KNEADING. WE INCLUDED THOSE AMOUNTS IN OUR RECIPES. UN-FORTUNATELY, THE ADDED LIQUID OFTEN CAUSES THE TOP OF THE BREAD TO SINK SLIGHTLY. IF YOU HAVE THE TIME AND PA-TIENCE TO EXPERIMENT, YOU MIGHT FIND YOU CAN ADJUST THOSE LIQUID AMOUNTS BY A TEASPOON OR SO TO PRODUCE A MORE ATTRACTIVE LOAF OF BREAD.

When a recipe calls for buttermilk, fresh is best. But for convenience, there's a dry buttermilk powder on the market that is an acceptable alternative. If your local grocer doesn't carry it, you will find it stocked at a natural-foods store. Keep it in the refrigerator.

Our recipes using buttermilk also list in parentheses the amount of butter-milk powder you can substitute. For example: 1⅛ cups buttermilk (or 5 tablespoons buttermilk powder and 1⅛ cups water). There's no need to mix the powder with water before adding it to the rest of the ingredients—just substitute 1⅛ cups water for the 1⅛ cups buttermilk and add the 5 tablespoons buttermilk powder along with the dry ingredients.

A similar substitution can be made if you find yourself out of milk. Add 1½ tablespoons nonfat dry milk powder to the 1½ pound loaf or 1 tablespoon powder for the 1-pound loaf.

Fresh buttermilk freezes well. We recommend freezing it in ⅞-, 1-, or 1⅛-cup quantities if you don't use it that often. When you know you're going to need it in a recipe, thaw it overnight in the refrigerator and then shake it very well before using.

Most recipes calling for buttermilk also list baking soda because it neutralizes the buttermilk's acidity. The same is usually true for sour cream.

FATS

Fats add flavor and tenderness, and keep the bread from turning stale rapidly. (Note that the Authentic French Bread, page 22, has no fat in the recipe. As a result, it dries out and loses its flavor in just a matter of hours.)

Margarine is fine to use but if you choose butter, select unsalted butter; it is usually fresher. Also, for your convenience, select a brand of butter that has tablespoon measurements marked on the wrapper; some don't. Do not substitute shortening for the butter or margarine unless the recipe specifically calls for it.

When a recipe calls for more than 2 tablespoons of butter, cut it into smaller pieces to ensure that it will blend well with the other ingredients.

SWEETENERS

Sweeteners such as granulated sugar, brown sugar, honey, molasses, corn syrup, or maple syrup add flavor and color to the crust and provide food for the yeast.

EGGS

Use only large eggs. One large egg is equivalent to a scant ¼ cup liquid and it will add a golden color and a cakelike texture to the loaf. To eliminate cholesterol, you can substitute ¼ cup water or ¼ cup liquid egg substitute or 2 egg whites for each egg.

SALT

You can omit the salt in the recipes if you are on a salt-restricted diet. However, the salt affects both the time it takes the dough to rise and the strength of the gluten formed. Your salt-free loaf will rise more rapidly but not as high, and will have a tendency to collapse. You might have to reduce the amount of liquid and yeast slightly. If the loaf still collapses, use a Rapid Bake setting. (Salt substitutes are unsatisfactory.)

Avoid adding the yeast directly on top of the salt or vice versa. The two don't mix. (This is not a problem for machines like the Panasonic/National, which drop the yeast automatically after the first kneading.)

YEAST

Yeast is a live fungus that feeds on sugar, fermenting it and producing carbon dioxide. Small bubbles of carbon dioxide are trapped in the gluten, the bread's structure, and as they expand, the bread rises. To avoid killing the yeast, do not use liquids that are extremely cold or hot.

IMPORTANT: SOME MACHINES REQUIRE MORE YEAST THAN OTHERS. WE HAVE LISTED THE PROPER YEAST AMOUNTS FOR EACH TYPE OF MACHINE IN EVERY RECIPE. TAKE CARE TO SELECT THE RIGHT AMOUNT FOR YOUR MACHINE.

In each recipe, yeast amounts for the 1½-pound loaf are listed under the categories of: All Machines, Welbilt/Dak, and Panasonic/National. If you are unsure which category your machine falls into, the following explanation should help:

ALL MACHINES	Hitachi, Sanyo, Maxim, Regal, Whole Wheat Panasonic/National or any machine with a basic white-bread recipe listing: 1⅛ cups liquid 3 cups flour 1½ teaspoons yeast
WELBILT/DAK	Welbilt, Dak, Zojirushi, or any machine with a basic white-bread recipe listing: 1¼ cups liquid 3 cups flour 1 package (2¼ teaspoons) yeast

If you are using the older 1½-pound Panasonic/National Model SD-BT6P you will get better results by doubling the yeast amounts called for in our recipes. Since the yeast dispenser has a limited capacity, you will find 4 to 4½ teaspoons of yeast will be the most you can use.

(*Note:* All 1-pound machines use the same amount of yeast in their basic white-bread recipes, so there is no need to categorize the machines for the 1-pound loaf size.)

Use packaged active dry yeast—regular, *not* rapid rise. We used Red Star brand active dry yeast when testing the recipes in this book and recommend it. After testing both Fleischmann's and Red Star active dry yeasts in various recipes, we discovered that the Fleischmann's yeast produced a significantly smaller loaf than the Red Star. If Red Star is not readily available, however, *Fleischmann's yeast can be substituted simply by adding another teaspoon of it to any recipe.* Or you can write to Universal Foods and order Red Star active dry yeast in bulk. The address is Universal Foods Corporation, 433 East Michigan Street, P.O. Box 737, Milwaukee, Wisconsin 53201.

We discovered a considerable savings in the cost of yeast by buying it in bulk at a local wholesale restaurant and janitorial supply store. Store the yeast in a covered container in the refrigerator. If you suspect your yeast has gone past its prime because your loaves aren't rising as high, test it by adding 1 teaspoon yeast and 1 tablespoon sugar to 1 cup warm water (105–115°F.) and wait five minutes. If the mixture doesn't start to foam slightly, your yeast has gotten old. Throw it out and buy some fresh yeast.

One last word about yeast: Feel free to experiment with the quantities of yeast listed in these recipes. We have a friend who, just on principle, throws an additional teaspoon of yeast into every loaf. So far she's had only one overflow. We encourage that attitude in everyone. These are fantastic, well-tested recipes but not everyone agrees on the "perfect" texture, density, or flavor of certain breads. A pinch more of this or that will make these recipes your own.

MISCELLANEOUS INGREDIENTS

For the best results, use the freshest ingredients. This is particularly true of things such as Parmesan cheese, as noted in the recipe for Anita's Italian Herb Bread on page 27.

Several recipes call for sunflower seeds. We found that raw, unsalted seeds from the natural-foods store bins were best.

When a recipe lists beer as an ingredient, use either flat beer or pour off the foamy head before measuring.

Potatoes, buttermilk, eggs, and oats add a wonderful rich flavor and moist texture to breads and rolls. Keep them in mind when you want to vary a recipe.

A NOTE FOR THOSE ON SPECIAL DIETS

If you are concerned about cholesterol, you can substitute nonfat milk for whole milk and two egg whites or ¼ cup water or ¼ cup liquid egg substitute for each egg.

If you are a vegetarian who eats no dairy products, you can substitute water or soymilk for the milk or buttermilk, ¼ cup water for each egg, vegetable shortening or oil for the butter or margarine.

MEASUREMENTS ◆◆◆◆◆◆◆◆◆◆◆◆◆◆◆◆◆◆◆◆◆◆◆

BASIC MEASUREMENTS

1½ teaspoons = ½ tablespoon
3 teaspoons = 1 tablespoon
4 tablespoons = ¼ cup
5⅓ tablespoons = ⅓ cup
16 tablespoons = 1 cup

You'll find that eighth-cup measures are frequently used in measuring liquids. The measuring cup that probably came with your machine is marked in eighths.

⅛ cup = 2 tablespoons

Therefore:

⅜ cup = ¼ cup + 2 tablespoons
⅝ cup = ½ cup + 2 tablespoons
⅞ cup = ¾ cup + 2 tablespoons
1⅛ cups = 1 cup + 2 tablespoons

TIPS FOR BAKING THE PERFECT LOAF ◆◆◆◆◆◆◆◆

There are several things we've learned along the way about bread machines and baking bread that we'd like to pass on to you:

▶ There is a significant difference between Red Star and Fleischmann's brands active dry yeast when used in the bread machine. We recommend Red Star brand yeast for the tallest loaves. An adequate substitution can be made, however, using an extra teaspoon of Fleischmann's yeast in any recipe.

▶ Experience will be your best teacher. If you're new at the bread-baking business, make a point of looking at the dough several times during the kneading process and while it is rising. (If you have a machine like the

Panasonic/National, avoid opening the lid when the yeast is about to drop from it.) You'll soon have a sense of the proper consistency for the perfect loaf. By checking the dough halfway through the mixing cycle, you can sometimes prevent a failure. If it appears too dry or wet, add more liquid or flour to correct it. Sometimes, all it takes is a tablespoon or two. If the mixing cycle is almost over, you can make the addition, stop the machine, and then restart it.

▶ You'll notice our recipe instructions include a descriptive box, such as:

```
CRUST: LIGHT
MENU SELECTION: BAKE (LIGHT)
```

The directions for the majority of the recipes are to place all ingredients in bread pan, select a crust setting, and press Start. The boxes will save you time because you can determine the menu settings at a glance. The actual menu settings are different for each machine. Should you have any doubt as to what the settings are for your machine, refer to this explanation:

FOR THE HITACHI, SANYO, REGAL, MAXIM MACHINES:

```
CRUST: REGULAR
MENU SELECTION: BAKE
```
= BREAD COLOR: REGULAR
  MENU: BREAD

```
CRUST: LIGHT
MENU SELECTION: BAKE (LIGHT)
```
= BREAD COLOR: LIGHT
  MENU: BREAD

```
MENU SELECTION: DOUGH
```
= MENU: DOUGH

```
CRUST: REGULAR
MENU SELECTION: RAPID BAKE
```
= BREAD COLOR: REGULAR
  MENU: BREAD RAPID

FOR THE PANASONIC/NATIONAL MACHINES:

```
CRUST: REGULAR
MENU SELECTION: BAKE
```
= SELECT: BAKE

```
CRUST: LIGHT
MENU SELECTION: BAKE (LIGHT)
```
= SELECT: BAKE (LIGHT)

```
MENU SELECTION: DOUGH
```
= SELECT: DOUGH

```
CRUST: REGULAR
MENU SELECTION: RAPID BAKE
```
= SELECT: BAKE (RAPID)

FOR THE WELBILT/DAK MACHINES:

CRUST: REGULAR MENU SELECTION: BAKE	=	CRUST: ADJUST TEMP. SENSOR TO MEDIUM SELECT: WHITE BREAD
CRUST: LIGHT MENU SELECTION: BAKE (LIGHT)	=	CRUST: ADJUST TEMPERATURE SENSOR TO LIGHT SELECT: WHITE BREAD
MENU SELECTION: DOUGH	=	SELECT: WHITE BREAD & MANUAL
CRUST: REGULAR MENU SELECTION: RAPID BAKE	=	N/A. NO RAPID BAKE SETTING.

(Some of our 1-pound loaf recipes require a Rapid Bake setting to prevent collapse. The 1-pound Welbilt machine has no Rapid Bake setting; however, that's not a problem since it bakes all loaves in just over two hours, which is the same as a rapid bake.)

▶ Any ingredients that are heated or cooked on the stove should be allowed to cool to room temperature before you add them to the rest of the ingredients; otherwise, they will kill the yeast. By the way, some bread-machine manufacturers recommend warming the liquids before combining them with the rest of the ingredients while others do not. Wanting to keep our methods as quick and easy as possible, we chose not to warm any liquids when several tests proved it didn't make a significant difference. We suggest, however, that you add the ingredients to the bread pan in the order listed to avoid placing the yeast in milk straight from the refrigerator.

▶ Store all whole-grain flours, bran, cracked wheat, bulgur, wheat germ, and nuts in sealed containers in the freezer to prevent them from turning rancid.

▶ If you plan to bake bread daily, make it as convenient for yourself as possible. We fill our canister sets with bread flour, sugar, nonfat dry milk powder, and oats. In the cupboard overhead we have containers of salt, honey, molasses, brown sugar, instant potato flakes, raisins, cornmeal, baking soda, herbs, and spices. With that arrangement, it's possible to toss together all the ingredients for a loaf of bread in just five minutes!

▶ If you like to bake a wide variety of breads, we suggest having these ingredients on hand:

FLOURS:	Bread, all-purpose (unbleached or regular), whole wheat, rye, barley, buckwheat, millet
LIQUIDS:	Milk or nonfat dry milk powder, buttermilk or dry buttermilk powder
WHOLE GRAINS	Oats, miller's bran, wheat germ, cracked wheat or bulgur, millet

SWEETENERS:	Granulated sugar, dark and light brown sugar, confectioners' sugar, honey, molasses
FATS:	Margarine or unsalted butter, vegetable and olive oil, shortening
MISCELLANEOUS:	Yeast, salt, instant potato flakes, eggs, sour cream, sunflower seeds, oranges, raisins, various herbs and spices

▶ All of our recipes can be baked in the oven instead of in the bread machine. For those who want to work the dough with their hands and bake a more traditional loaf, we suggest you place the ingredients in the bread pan and set the machine on Dough. When it beeps that it's done, turn the dough out onto a floured countertop and knead it for one or two minutes. Place the 1½-pound loaf in a greased 9 × 5 × 3-inch loaf pan. Place the 1-pound loaf in a greased 8½ × 4½ × 2½-inch loaf pan. (Or, in the case of a rye or pumpernickel bread, shape the dough into a round or oblong loaf and place it on a greased baking sheet.) Cover and let rise in a warm place until doubled, 30 to 45 minutes. You can bake most loaves at 375°F. for 35 to 45 minutes until golden brown.

▶ To achieve nice, rounded tops on loaves baked in the 1½-pound Welbilt/Dak machine, you have to *omit* the recommended additional 1 to 2 tablespoons of liquid. We hesitate to suggest doing so because the few times we tried it, the machine seemed to struggle with the stiffer dough. Though most loaves baked with the recommended additional water have sunken tops, on the plus side, they usually have a superior texture and a tender crumb.

▶ We had problems with several of the sweeter breads burning in the 1½-pound Welbilt/Dak machine. Setting the crust control on the lightest setting resulted in a layer of raw dough on top. We had more success baking them on Sweet Bread, using a Medium to Light Crust setting.

▶ We've noticed that in the rectangular pans (they're wider than they are tall, such as the 1½-pound Panasonic/National bread pan), sometimes it is necessary to push some of the ingredients out of the corners with a rubber spatula during the mixing cycle to ensure proper blending. Also, the same pan will occasionally produce a very odd-looking loaf that resembles a ski slope—very high at one end and quite low at the other. We believe that happens on those rare occasions when the dough ends up on one side of the pan after the final kneading and doesn't rise properly. Again, moving the dough with a rubber spatula at that point will prevent it.

▶ If a recipe calls for both oil and honey or molasses, measure the oil first. The honey or molasses will then slide easily out of the tablespoon.

▶ To make use of the last few drops of honey or molasses that coat the sides of the jar, remove the lid and place the jar in the microwave on High for 10 to 15 seconds. It will then pour easily into your measuring spoon.

▶ When a recipe calls for more than 2 tablespoons of butter, cut it into small pieces to ensure proper blending.

- Most machines have a timer for delayed baking. As probably noted in your instructions, be careful not to use anything that might spoil when using the timer, such as eggs, milk, sour cream, cottage cheese, and buttermilk. Add the ingredients in the order listed to prevent the yeast from sitting in the liquid for hours.

- Once a loaf is done, remove it from the bread pan as soon as possible. Left to sit in the bread pan for long, it will turn damp and soggy on the outside.

- Once in a while you'll have loaves that turn out like mini-boulders rather than anything edible. Did you forget to place the blade securely in the machine? Did you forget to add the yeast? Chances are, you probably added too much flour or not enough liquid. Toss the loaf out (watch where you aim it!) and try again.

- Too much liquid in the dough can produce a wide variety of results. It will usually cause a whole-grain loaf to be coarse and full of holes, or very small, with a flat or sunken top. A tall loaf that is spongy-soft with caved-in sides or breads that rise too high and mushroom over the top of the bread pan also have too much liquid in the dough; reducing the liquid by 2 tablespoons usually solves the problem. Don't forget that ingredients such as fruits, vegetables, sour cream, and cottage cheese add moisture to the dough as well.

- If a loaf consistently rises too fast but looks very deflated after it bakes, that means it had too long a rising period. The gluten strands broke, the gas escaped, and the bread fell while baking. Use the Rapid Bake setting for that particular recipe.

- Use the Light Crust setting for recipes that call for whole grains, cheese, eggs, or extra sugar.

- You may notice that some recipes require all-purpose flour for the 1½-pound machine and bread flour for the 1-pound machine or vice versa. We had to switch to the all-purpose for that particular loaf because in our testings it rose too high with the bread flour.

- There may be a day when you bake your favorite loaf, the one that's been a proven success time after time, and, incredibly, it turns out to be a dud! You *know* you followed the recipe exactly. What happened? Blame it on the weather—that's the best we can tell you. On those days when the humidity is either very high or low, the flour's ability to absorb moisture changes. It happens to everyone, so don't get discouraged. It may not look like a winner but, chances are, it will still taste fine. (To prevent such an occurrence, as the dough is mixing add one or two more tablespoons flour on very humid days. For those dry, dry days, increase the liquid by two or three teaspoons.)

- A good serrated bread knife is invaluable! Fortunately, some machines come with one. If yours didn't, make it your first purchase.

- A plastic measuring cup is provided with some machines and the lines on

10

it are difficult to read. Lois uses a permanent-ink marking pen to highlight the measurement line she needs. The markings will wash off.

▶ Here's a tip from one who learned the hard way: Remember to remove the mixing blade from that special loaf of bread you've baked as a gift. Once wrapped and given, it's quite embarrassing to ask for it back!

▶ If you are working with a very sticky dough when making rolls or a specialty bread, simply knead in a little more flour until the dough is easier to handle.

▶ When you make rolls or any of the specialty breads that call for shaping the dough by hand and letting it rise in a warm place, we've discovered that if you simply turn on your oven to the lowest setting (Warm) for two minutes, then turn it off, and place the covered dough in the warm oven for 30 to 45 minutes, the dough rises beautifully.

▶ If you're making rolls or specialty breads and the recipe calls for a baking pan or a cake pan, and all you have is a glass baking dish or pie plate, reduce the oven temperature by 25°F. to avoid overbrowning.

▶ Dark pans will produce dark crusts; shiny pans will produce lighter crusts.

▶ When making sweet rolls that are rolled up jelly-roll fashion and then sliced, try using dental floss or heavy thread instead of a knife to cut the dough. (Using a knife to cut the roll usually squashes it.) Lightly mark the roll with a knife where you want it sliced. Starting at one end, slide a 12-inch length of dental floss or heavy thread underneath the roll and at each mark, bring the ends of the floss up and crisscross them at the top of the roll. Pull in opposite directions until the floss cuts through the roll completely.

▶ You can store bread dough that you can't bake right away, by either putting it in a covered container or dusting it with flour and putting it in a plastic bag, then placing it in the refrigerator for a day or two. Allow it to come to room temperature before shaping it into a loaf or rolls. To store it longer than a day or two, shape the dough into a loaf or rolls, wrap it well in plastic and foil, label, and freeze up to one month. Remove from the freezer about six hours before serving time (three hours for rolls). After it defrosts completely, let the dough rise 30 to 45 minutes in a warm place until doubled in size, then bake as directed in the recipe.

▶ Baked bread and rolls, if allowed to cool *completely* and wrapped well in plastic, foil, or plastic bags, can be refrigerated for one week or frozen satisfactorily for one month. (It's best to slice the bread first if you plan on using only one slice at a time.) It will thaw at room temperature in approximately 30 minutes. To thaw a slice or a roll quickly, microwave it on High power for 15 to 20 seconds. Avoid over-zapping it; you'll end up with bread hard as a rock when it cools.

▶ The next question that arises, once you find your freezer half full of bags containing that one last slice of bread no one will kill off, is what to do with all those odds and ends. First, you should know that you will never again have to buy bread crumbs. A quick whirl in the food processor will turn those orphan slices into the most delicious bread crumbs imaginable! With not much more effort, you can create some delicious croutons that will make your salads sparkle! (See our recipes for Croutons on page 181.) Bread pudding and french toast made with many of the breads in this cookbook will leave the realm of ordinary and achieve memorable status. New on the market this past year is a snack-making appliance that turns a couple slices of bread and various fillings into just about any snack imaginable. What could be more perfect! Finally, if you're overworked, stressed out, and can't be bothered to make use of any of the preceding suggestions, here's the best one of all: Dump all those stray slices into one bag, visit your own backyard or the nearest park, and take a few moments' time out to do something nice for your neighborhood birds, ducks, or squirrels. Your day will be brighter for it.

▶ Last and most important, have fun with this fabulous new appliance! Experiment with new shapes and taste sensations. You can turn a plain dough into a masterpiece by braiding it, brushing it with egg white, and sprinkling poppy or sesame seeds on top. How about sculpting a bread basket simply by twining ropes of bread dough around the outside of an inverted, greased bowl? After baking, remove the bowl and you have a lovely basket for your homemade rolls. We know of one talented lady who combined several batches of dough and created a cornucopia using a similar method. She shaped the basic cornucopia form from wadded-up aluminum foil, greased it well, and then wrapped her ropes of dough around it. The last coils around the opening were braided for a finished look. For the final step, she glazed it with egg white, baked it, and then removed the foil once it cooled. As you can imagine, filled with a variety of fresh rolls, it was a show stopper! If you're not feeling quite that inspired, have fun just shaping small, individual bread bowls the next time you serve chili or stew to family or friends. One large, round loaf hollowed out and toasted in a 350°F. oven is a tasty container for your favorite dip or fondue. Experiment with various cooking containers such as coffee cans and clay flower pots. See how much fun you can have with just a little imagination! Who knows, you might come up with a bake-off winner or a blue ribbon at a state fair. We wish you luck!—Linda Rehberg
Lois Conway
www.breadmachinemagic.com

WHITE BREADS

✦✦ BASIC WHITE BREAD ✦✦

This is a very basic recipe for white bread and probably similar to the one that comes with your machine. It's a good place to start—the ingredients are readily available and it's a nicely shaped loaf of bread.

1½-POUND LOAF

½ cup water (for Welbilt/Dak
  machines add 2 tablespoons
  more water)
⅝ cup milk
3 cups bread flour
1½ teaspoons salt
1½ tablespoons butter or
  margarine
3 tablespoons sugar
1½ teaspoons Red Star brand
  active dry yeast for all
  machines except1½-pound
  Welbilt/Dak machines (use 2
  teaspoons yeast)

1-POUND LOAF

½ cup water (for Welbilt
  machine no extra water is
  needed)
⅜ cup milk
2 cups bread flour
1 teaspoon salt
1 tablespoon butter or
  margarine
2 tablespoons sugar
1½ teaspoons Red Star brand
  active dry yeast for all
  machines

Place all ingredients in bread pan and press Start.

After the baking cycle ends, remove bread from pan, place on cake rack, and allow to cool 1 hour before slicing.

CRUST: REGULAR
MENU SELECTION: BAKE

•• BROWN BAGGER'S ••
WHITE BREAD

For sandwiches we often use this hearty white bread because it holds up well in a lunchbox or picnic basket.

1½-POUND LOAF

½ cup milk

½ cup water (for Welbilt/Dak machines add 2 tablespoons more water)

1 egg

3 cups bread flour

3 tablespoons wheat germ

2 tablespoons instant potato flakes

1½ teaspoons salt

1½ tablespoons oil

3 tablespoons sugar

1½ teaspoons Red Star brand active dry yeast for all machines except 1½-pound Welbilt/Dak machines (use 2 teaspoons yeast)

1-POUND LOAF

⅜ cup milk

⅜ cup water (for Welbilt machine no extra water is needed)

1 egg

2 cups bread flour

2 tablespoons wheat germ

1 tablespoon instant potato flakes

1 teaspoon salt

1 tablespoon oil

2 tablespoons sugar

1½ teaspoons Red Star brand active dry yeast for all machines

Place all ingredients in bread pan, select Light Crust setting, and press Start.

After the baking cycle ends, remove bread from pan, place on cake rack, and allow to cool 1 hour before slicing.

CRUST: LIGHT
MENU SELECTION: BAKE (LIGHT)

◆◆ DEDE'S BUTTERMILK BREAD ◆◆

If Linda's sister DeDe ever breaks down and buys a bread machine, it will be because of this moist, rich, and tender loaf. Plain, white sandwich bread doesn't get much better than this!

1½-POUND LOAF	1-POUND LOAF
1⅛ cups buttermilk (or 4 tablespoons dry buttermilk powder and 1⅛ cups water) (for Welbilt/Dak machines add 2 tablespoons more buttermilk)	⅞ cup buttermilk (or 3 tablespoons dry buttermilk powder and ⅞ cup water) (for Welbilt machine add 1 tablespoon more buttermilk)
3 cups bread flour	2 cups bread flour
1½ teaspoons salt	1 teaspoon salt
1 tablespoon butter or margarine	1 tablespoon butter or margarine
3 tablespoons honey	2 tablespoons honey
¼ teaspoon baking soda	¼ teaspoon baking soda
1½ teaspoons Red Star brand active dry yeast for all machines except 1½-pound Welbilt/Dak machines (use 2 teaspoons yeast)	1½ teaspoons Red Star brand active dry yeast for all machines

Place all ingredients in bread pan, select Light Crust setting, and press Start.

After the baking cycle ends, remove bread from pan, place on cake rack, and allow to cool 1 hour before slicing.

CRUST: LIGHT
MENU SELECTION: BAKE (LIGHT)

◆◆ EGG BREAD ◆◆

Need a bread for sandwiches? Here's the perfect companion for anything from tuna to cheese. The eggs give it a rich, velvety taste and texture. We like to keep a loaf in the freezer for Sunday morning's french toast.

1½-POUND LOAF

¾ cup milk (for Welbilt/Dak machines add 2 tablespoons more milk)

2 eggs

3 cups bread flour

1½ teaspoons salt

3 tablespoons butter or margarine

¼ cup sugar

1½ teaspoons Red Star brand active dry yeast for all machines except 1½-pound Welbilt/Dak machines (use 2 teaspoons yeast)

1-POUND LOAF

½ cup milk (for Welbilt machine add 3 tablespoons more milk)

1 egg

2 cups bread flour

1 teaspoon salt

2 tablespoons butter or margarine

3 tablespoons sugar

1½ teaspoons Red Star brand active dry yeast for all machines

Place all ingredients in bread pan, select Light Crust setting, and press Start.

After the baking cycle ends, remove bread from pan, place on cake rack, and allow to cool 1 hour before slicing.

CRUST: LIGHT
MENU SELECTION: BAKE (LIGHT)

◆◆ IRISH POTATO BREAD ◆◆

We tested several potato breads and this one was by far the best. It is soft and spongy and has a wonderful flavor.

1½-POUND LOAF

⅝ cup milk
¼ cup potato water* (for Welbilt/Dak machines add 2 tablespoons more potato water)
3 cups all-purpose flour
⅓ cup plain mashed potato, at room temperature
1½ teaspoons salt
1½ tablespoons butter or margarine
1½ tablespoons sugar
1½ teaspoons Red Star brand active dry yeast for all machines except 1½-pound Welbilt/Dak machines (use 2 teaspoons yeast)

1-POUND LOAF

⅜ cup milk
¼ cup potato water* (for Welbilt machine add 1 tablespoon more potato water)
2 cups all-purpose flour
¼ cup plain mashed potato, at room temperature
1 teaspoon salt
1 tablespoon butter or margarine
1 tablespoon sugar
1½ teaspoons Red Star brand active dry yeast for all machines

Place all ingredients in a bread pan, select Light Crust setting, and press Start.

After the baking cycle ends, remove bread from pan, place on cake rack, and allow to cool 1 hour before slicing.

```
CRUST: LIGHT
MENU SELECTION: BAKE (LIGHT)
```

*The water in which you cooked the potato.

✦ LINDA'S EASY POTATO BREAD ✦

This bread is moist and fluffy and a family favorite for sandwiches. (Note: The 1-pound loaf is baked on the Rapid Bake setting to prevent it from overflowing the pan.)

1½-POUND LOAF

¼ cup instant potato flakes
¾ cup milk
⅜ cup water (for Welbilt/Dak machines add 3 tablespoons more water)
3 cups bread flour
1½ teaspoons salt
1½ tablespoons butter or margarine
1½ tablespoons sugar
2 teaspoons Red Star brand active dry yeast for all machines

1-POUND LOAF

3 tablespoons instant potato flakes
½ cup milk
⅜ cup water (for Welbilt machine add 1 tablespoon more water)
2 cups bread flour
1 teaspoon salt
1 tablespoon butter or margarine
1 tablespoon sugar
1½ teaspoons Red Star brand active dry yeast for all machines

FOR 1½-POUND LOAF

Place all ingredients in bread pan, select Light Crust setting, and press Start.

After the baking cycle ends, remove bread from pan, place on cake rack, and allow to cool 1 hour before slicing.

| CRUST: LIGHT |
| MENU SELECTION: BAKE (LIGHT) |

FOR 1-POUND LOAF

Place all ingredients in bread pan, select Rapid Bake setting, and press Start.

After the baking cycle ends, remove bread from pan, place on cake rack, and allow to cool 1 hour before slicing.

| CRUST: REGULAR |
| MENU SELECTION: RAPID BAKE |

✦✦ MIDNIGHT-SUN BREAD ✦✦

This is an outstanding bread! It has a delicate, cake-like texture and combines the orange and caraway flavors that are popular in so many Scandinavian breads. It's also good toasted.

1½-POUND LOAF

1⅛ cups buttermilk (or 4
  tablespoons dry buttermilk
  powder and 1⅛ cup water)
  (for Welbilt/Dak machines add
  2 tablespoons more
  buttermilk)
3 cups bread flour
1½ teaspoons salt
2 tablespoons butter or
  margarine
2 tablespoons honey
Grated rind of 1 small orange
1½ teaspoons caraway seeds
½ cup raisins
2 teaspoons Red Star brand
  active dry yeast for all
  machines

1-POUND LOAF

¾ cup buttermilk (or 3
  tablespoons dry buttermilk
  powder and ¾ cup water)
  (for Welbilt machine add 1
  tablespoon more buttermilk)
2 cups bread flour
1 teaspoon salt
1½ tablespoons butter or
  margarine
1½ tablespoons honey
Granted rind of ½ orange
1 teaspoon caraway seeds
⅓ cup raisins
1½ teaspoons Red Star brand
  active dry yeast for all
  machines

Place all ingredients in bread pan, select Light Crust setting, and press Start.

After the baking cycle ends, remove bread from pan, place on cake rack, and allow to cool 1 hour before slicing.

CRUST: LIGHT
MENU SELECTION: BAKE (LIGHT)

❖❖ ENGLISH TOASTING BREAD ❖❖

This is a special bread, coated with cornmeal, so it needs to be baked in a loaf pan in the oven. It's heavenly with orange marmalade.

1½-POUND LOAF	1-POUND LOAF
¾ cup milk	⅝ cup milk
⅜ cup water (for Welbilt/Dak machines add 2 tablespoons more water)	¼ cup water (for Welbilt machine add 1 tablespoon more water)
3 cups bread flour	2 cups bread flour
1 teaspoon salt	½ teaspoon salt
2 teaspoons sugar	1½ teaspoons sugar
¼ teaspoon baking soda	¼ teaspoon baking soda
2 teaspoons Red Star brand active dry yeast for all machines	2 teaspoons Red Star brand active dry yeast for all machines
Cornmeal	Cornmeal

Place all ingredients except cornmeal in a bread pan, select Dough setting, and press Start.

When dough has risen long enough, the machine will beep. Turn off bread machine, remove bread pan, and turn out dough onto a floured countertop or cutting board.

Grease an 8½ × 4½ × 2½-inch loaf pan; sprinkle all sides with cornmeal. Place dough into prepared loaf pan. With your hands, carefully press it evenly into pan. Sprinkle the top with cornmeal. Cover and let rise in a warm oven for 20 to 30 minutes or until dough almost reaches the top of the pan. (Hint: To warm oven slightly, turn oven on Warm setting for 2 minutes, then turn it off, and place covered dough in oven to rise. Remove pan from oven to preheat.)

Preheat oven to 400°F. Bake for 25 minutes. Remove from oven; remove loaf from pan and cool on wire rack. To serve, cut into thick slices and toast.

```
MENU SELECTION: DOUGH
```

•• AUTHENTIC FRENCH BREAD ••

This fine-tasting bread is a fixture at our dinner parties. Since it contains no fat, it starts to go stale in just a matter of hours. Plan to serve this bread shortly after it comes out of the oven. Set a tub of sweet, creamery butter next to it and watch the loaf disappear!

1½-POUND LOAF

1 cup water (for Welbilt/Dak
   machines add 2 tablespoons
   more water)
1½ teaspoons salt
3 cups bread flour
2 teaspoons Red Star brand
   active dry yeast for all
   machines
Cornmeal

1-POUND LOAF

¾ cup water (for Welbilt/Dak
   machine add 1 tablespoon
   more water)
1 teaspoon salt
2 cups bread flour
2 teaspoons Red Star brand
   active dry yeast for all
   machines
Cornmeal

Place all ingredients except cornmeal in bread pan, select Dough setting, and press Start.

When dough has risen long enough, the machine will beep. Turn off bread machine, remove bread pan, and turn out dough onto a floured countertop or cutting board.

FOR 1½-POUND LOAF

Shape dough into one 12-inch oblong loaf or 1 large round loaf or two 18-inch thin baguettes or 8 French rolls.

FOR 1-POUND LOAF

Shape dough into one 10-inch oblong loaf or 1 large round loaf or one 24-inch thin baguette or 6 French rolls.

Dust the top(s) with a little flour; rub it in. Place the loaves on a cookie sheet dusted with cornmeal. With a very sharp knife or razor blade, slash the tops of the rolls or baguettes straight down the center about ½ inch deep. On the oblong loaf, make 3 diagonal slashes. On the round loaf, slash an X or # on top. Cover and let rise in a warm oven for 30 to 45 minutes until doubled. (Hint: To warm oven slightly, turn oven on Warm setting for 2 minutes, then turn it off, and place covered dough in oven to rise. Remove pan from oven to preheat.)

Place a pan of hot water on the bottom rack of the oven. (This will create steam, which is necessary to produce an authentic, crisp crust.) Preheat oven to 450°F. Bake the round or oblong loaves about 20 minutes, the baguettes about 15 minutes, and the rolls 10 to 12 minutes. Remove from oven; cool on a wire rack. This is best served within hours of baking. To preserve the crisp crust, do not store in plastic wrap or bags.

MENU SELECTION: DOUGH

·· ANADAMA BREAD ··

There's a story that goes along with this classic bread, which dates back to colonial times. A cantankerous New England backwoodsman had a very lazy wife, named Anna, who fed him nothing but cornmeal mush for supper. Night after night cornmeal mush until one evening he couldn't take it any more. He grabbed some flour, molasses, and yeast off the shelf, stirred it into his mush, and put it in the fire to bake. As the loaf baked, he muttered over and over, "Anna, damn her!"

1½-POUND LOAF

1¼ cups water (for Welbilt/Dak machines no extra water is needed)
3 cups bread flour
⅓ cup yellow cornmeal
1½ teaspoons salt
1½ tablespoons butter or margarine
3 tablespoons molasses
1½ teaspoons Red Star brand active dry yeast for all machines except 1½-pound Welbilt/Dak machines (use 2 teaspoons yeast)

1-POUND LOAF

¾ cup water (for Welbilt machine add 1 tablespoon more water)
2 cups bread flour
¼ cup yellow cornmeal
1 teaspoon salt
1 tablespoon butter or margarine
2 tablespoons molasses
1½ teaspoons Red Star brand active dry yeast for all machines

Place all ingredients in bread pan and press Start.

After the baking cycle ends, remove bread from pan, place on cake rack, and allow to cool 1 hour before slicing.

CRUST: REGULAR
MENU SELECTION: BAKE

◆◆ TANGY BUTTERMILK ◆◆ CHEESE BREAD

This is a tangy, tender bread. Use extra-sharp cheese for the best flavor.

1½-POUND LOAF

1⅛ cups buttermilk (or 4
  tablespoons dry buttermilk
  powder and 1⅛ cups water)
  (For Welbilt/Dak machines
  add 2 tablespoons more
  buttermilk)
3 cups bread flour
1½ teaspoons salt
1½ tablespoons sugar
¾ cup (3 ounces) grated extra-
  sharp Cheddar cheese
1½ teaspoons Red Star brand
  active dry yeast for all
  machines except 1½-pound
  Welbilt/Dak machines (use 2
  teaspoons yeast)

1-POUND LOAF

⅞ cup buttermilk (or 3
  tablespoons dry buttermilk
  powder and ⅞ cup water)
  (For Welbilt machine no extra
  buttermilk is needed)
2 cups bread flour
1 teaspoon salt
1 tablespoon sugar
½ cup (2 ounces) grated extra-
  sharp Cheddar cheese
1½ teaspoons Red Star brand
  active dry yeast for all
  machines

Place all ingredients in bread pan, select Light Crust setting, and press Start.

After the baking cycle ends, remove bread from pan, place on cake rack, and allow to cool 1 hour before slicing.

CRUST: LIGHT
MENU SELECTION: BAKE (LIGHT)

·· HERB BREAD ··

Plan to be around while this one bakes, because the aroma is absolutely out of this world! As for the taste, it's hard to limit yourself to just one slice of this zesty bread. We recommend it for croutons, also. (Note: When making the 1-pound loaf, use the Rapid Bake setting for a better shaped bread.)

1½-POUND LOAF	1-POUND LOAF
3 tablespoons butter or margarine	2 tablespoons butter or margarine
½ cup chopped onion	⅓ cup chopped onion
1 cup milk (for Welbilt/Dak machines add 2 tablespoons more milk)	¾ cup milk (for Welbilt machine add 1 tablespoon more milk)
3 cups bread flour	2 cups bread flour
1½ teaspoons salt	1 teaspoon salt
1½ tablespoons sugar	1 tablespoon sugar
½ teaspoon dried dill	½ teaspoon dried dill
½ teaspoon dried basil	½ teaspoon dried basil
½ teaspoon dried rosemary	½ teaspoon dried rosemary
1½ teaspoons Red Star brand active dry yeast for all machines except 1½-pound Welbilt/Dak machines (use 2 teaspoons yeast)	1½ teaspoons Red Star brand active dry yeast for all machines

In a small skillet, melt butter over low heat. Add onion and sauté 8 to 10 minutes until onion is soft but not brown. Remove from heat; allow mixture to cool for 10 minutes before adding it to the bread pan.

FOR 1½-POUND LOAF

Place all ingredients including onion mixture in bread pan, select Light Crust setting, and press Start.

After the baking cycle ends, remove bread from pan, place on cake rack, and allow to cool 1 hour before slicing.

```
CRUST: LIGHT
MENU SELECTION: BAKE (LIGHT)
```

FOR 1-POUND LOAF

Place all ingredients including onion mixture in bread pan, select Rapid Bake setting, and press Start.

After the baking cycle ends, remove bread from pan, place on cake rack, and allow to cool 1 hour before slicing.

```
CRUST: REGULAR
MENU SELECTION: RAPID BAKE
```

✦✦ L & L BAKERS' DILL BREAD ✦✦

The virtue of this bread is its pungent herb and onion flavor and very light texture. In addition, it holds a special significance for us. It was such a big hit as a gift that it eventually became the starting point for this cookbook. We urge you to give this as a gift and see what good fortune awaits you, too.

1½-POUND LOAF
¼ cup milk
¼ cup water (for Welbilt/Dak/Zoji machines add 2 tablespoons more water)
1 egg
3 cups bread flour
1½ teaspoons salt
1½ tablespoons butter or margarine
3 tablespoons sugar
⅔ cup lowfat cottage cheese
2 tablespoons dried minced onion
1 tablespoon dried dill weed
1 tablespoon dried parsley flakes
1½ teaspoons Red Star brand active dry yeast for all machines except 1½-pound Welbilt/Dak machines (use 2 teaspoons yeast)

1-POUND LOAF
3 tablespoons milk
3 tablespoons water (for Welbilt/Zoji machines add 1 tablespoon more water)
1 egg
2 cups bread flour
1 teaspoon salt
1 tablespoon butter or margarine
2 tablespoons sugar
⅓ cup lowfat cottage cheese
1 tablespoon dried minced onion
2 teaspoons dried dill weed
2 teaspoons dried parsley flakes
2 teaspoons Red Star brand active dry yeast for all machines

Place all ingredients in bread pan, select Light Crust setting, and press Start.

After the baking cycle ends, remove bread from pan, place on cake rack, and allow to cool 1 hour before slicing.

```
CRUST: LIGHT
MENU SELECTION: BAKE (LIGHT)
```

✦✦ ANITA'S ITALIAN HERB BREAD ✦✦

For the best results, use the finest and freshest ingredients available. That is especially true for this particular recipe. Lois's sister Anita, who loves Italian food, will tell you that this fabulous bread is well worth the trip to your nearest Italian market or deli to purchase a chunk of imported Parmesan. You'll be disappointed with anything less, once you've tried it.

1½-POUND LOAF

1⅛ cups buttermilk (or 4 tablespoons dry buttermilk powder and 1⅛ cup water) (for Welbilt/Dak machines add 2 tablespoons more buttermilk)

3 cups bread flour

1½ teaspoons salt

1½ tablespoons oil

1 tablespoon sugar

½ cup (2 ounces) freshly grated imported Parmesan cheese

¼ teaspoon dried basil

¼ teaspoon dried oregano

1½ teaspoons Red Star brand active dry yeast for all machines except 1½-pound Welbilt/Dak machines (use 2 teaspoons yeast)

1-POUND LOAF

⅞ cup buttermilk (or 3 tablespoons dry buttermilk powder and ⅞ cup water) (for Welbilt machine add 1 tablespoon more buttermilk)

2 cups bread flour

1 teaspoon salt

1 tablespoon oil

2 teaspoons sugar

⅓ cup (1½ ounces) freshly grated imported Parmesan cheese

¼ teaspoon dried basil

¼ teaspoon dried oregano

1½ teaspoons Red Star brand active dry yeast for all machines

Place all ingredients in bread pan, select Light Crust setting, and press Start.

After the baking cycle ends, remove bread from pan, place on cake rack, and allow to cool 1 hour before slicing.

```
CRUST: LIGHT
MENU SELECTION: BAKE (LIGHT)
```

✦✦ SOURDOUGH MADE EASY ✦✦

We condensed the many pages of sourdough data we had compiled into this brief instruction and fact sheet. If you follow the steps carefully, you can produce your first loaf of delicious sourdough bread within a week. Good luck!

SOURDOUGH STARTER

1. Heat 1 cup skim (nonfat) milk to 90–100°F.
2. Stir in 3 tablespoons plain, fresh, high-quality yogurt.
3. Pour mixture into a 1-quart glass or ceramic crock, jar, or bowl. Cover with a nonmetallic lid; set in a warm place (70–100°F.) for 24 hours. (On a warm day you can place the starter outside in the sun or on the kitchen counter. On cooler days, place it in a gas oven with a pilot light, on top of the water heater, or on a heating pad set on low.)
4. After 24 hours, the milk will thicken and form curds. At this point, gradually stir in 1 cup all-purpose flour until well blended. Cover with lid and set in a warm place again until it ferments and bubbles and a clear liquid forms on top, about 2 to 5 days. Stir daily.
5. Starter is now ready to use. Stir, cover loosely, and refrigerate.

IF AT ANY POINT IN THE PROCESS THE STARTER TURNS PINK, SMELLS RANCID (NOT JUST SOUR), OR DEVELOPS A MOLD, THROW IT OUT AND START OVER.

REPLENISHING THE STARTER

Every time you use some of the starter you must replace it with a like amount of milk and flour. For instance, if you use 1 cup of starter, return 1 cup of milk and 1 cup of flour to the jar. Follow the directions for feeding the starter.

FEEDING THE STARTER TO KEEP IT ALIVE AND HEALTHY

A starter should be used as often as possible, at least every 2 to 3 weeks. If you are not using it that often, plan to feed it once a month to keep it going.
1. Bring the starter to room temperature. (You can place it in a bowl of warm water to speed the process.)
2. Add equal amounts of warm milk (90–100°F.) and flour (½ to 1 cup each).
3. Cover with lid and allow to stand in a warm place (70–100°F.) for 12 to 24 hours or until bubbly and a clear liquid has formed on top.
4. Stir, cover loosely (set lid on jar but do not tightly seal; gases must be allowed to escape), and refrigerate.

REJUVENATING A NEGLECTED STARTER

If you forget to feed your starter monthly, don't throw it away thinking it's gone bad. Chances are you can still revive it.
1. Pour off the liquid and discard all but 1 to 2 tablespoons of the starter. Temporarily place reserved starter in a bowl.

2. Wash out the starter container with hot water.
3. Put the starter back into the container.
4. Follow the directions for feeding the starter using 1 cup warm (90–100°F.) skim (nonfat) milk and 1 cup flour.
5. You may have to repeat this procedure once or twice to bring it back up to a bubbly, sour-smelling starter again.

SOURDOUGH FACTS TO KEEP IN MIND

▶ Use only wooden utensils and glass or ceramic containers. The acid in the starter will corrode any metal with which it comes in contact.

▶ Store loosely covered in the refrigerator; do not put in a tightly sealed container. The gases must be allowed to escape.

▶ The yellowish or grayish-beige liquid that rises to the top is the "hooch." Just stir it back in before measuring out starter for a recipe.

▶ You can refresh your starter once a year or so with a few tablespoons of fresh, plain, good-quality yogurt.

▶ For the sourest taste when making bread, mix the room-temperature starter with the liquid and half the flour called for in the recipe. Cover and allow to stand in a warm place until bubbly and very sour smelling, about 12 to 24 hours. At that point, combine the mixture in the bread machine with the rest of the ingredients in the recipe. Your starter can be frozen for up to 3 months. Before using it again, let it thaw completely at room temperature for 24 hours until bubbly. You may need to feed it once to bring it back to the bubbly stage after freezing.

We have included a recipe for a San Francisco-type Sourdough French Bread. However, we feel you could create some unique breads by using your starter in other recipes such as Tangy Buttermilk Cheese Bread, Basic Whole Wheat Bread, Lois's Rye Bread, Russian Black Bread, Apple Oatmeal Bread with Raisins, Dinner Rolls, Squaw Bread, Hamburger Buns, and English Muffins, just to name a few. Simply add ½ cup to 1 cup of the starter, as desired, to the recipe and decrease the liquid by approximately half the amount of starter used. (Example: Use ½ cup starter—decrease the liquid by ¼ cup.)

◆◆ "SAN FRANCISCO" ◆◆
SOURDOUGH FRENCH BREAD

Most people love the tangy, tart taste of sourdough. If you can't get to San Francisco for the real thing, this will do in a pinch. (Note: Starters vary in their consistency. If you find the dough very wet and sticky when you turn it out of the machine, simply knead in enough flour to make it easy to handle and hold its shape when formed into a loaf.)

1½-POUND LOAF	1-POUND LOAF
⅝ cup water (for Welbilt/Dak machines no extra water is / needed)	⅜ cup water (for Welbilt machine no extra water is needed)
1 cup sourdough starter (see Sourdough Made Easy, page 28)	¾ cup sourdough starter (see Sourdough Made Easy, page 28)
3 cups bread flour	2 cups bread flour
1 teaspoon salt	1 teaspoon salt
1 teaspoon sugar	1 teaspoon sugar
2 teaspoons Red Star brand active dry yeast for all machines	2 teaspoons Red Star brand active dry yeast for all machines
Cornmeal (optional)	Cornmeal (optional)

FOR A MILD SOURDOUGH

Place all ingredients except cornmeal in bread pan, insert pan into machine, select Dough setting, and press Start.

FOR THE SOUREST SOURDOUGH

In a medium bowl, combine the water, starter (room temperature), and half of the flour. Cover and let stand in a warm place until very sour and bubbly, from 12 to 24 hours. Then combine mixture with the rest of the ingredients except cornmeal in bread pan, insert pan into machine, select Dough setting, and press Start.

When dough has risen long enough, the machine will beep. Turn off bread machine, remove bread pan, and turn out dough onto a floured countertop or cutting board.

FOR 1½-POUND LOAF

Shape dough into one 12-inch oblong loaf or 1 round loaf or two 18-inch thin baguettes or 8 French rolls.

FOR 1-POUND LOAF

Shape dough into one 10-inch oblong loaf or 1 large round loaf or one 24-inch thin baguette or 6 French rolls.

Place loaf (loaves) on a baking sheet that is well greased or sprinkled with cornmeal. With a sharp knife or razor blade, slash the rolls or the baguettes straight down the center about ½ inch deep. On the oblong loaf, make three diagonal slashes. On the round loaf, slash an X or # on top. Let rise in warm oven 30 to 45 minutes until doubled. (Hint: To warm oven slightly, turn oven on Warm for 2 minutes, then turn it off, and place covered dough in oven to rise. Remove pan from oven to preheat it.)

Preheat oven to 400°F. With a plant mister, mist each loaf with water (or brush with water). Bake 25 to 30 minutes until golden brown, misting with water twice more at 5-minute intervals. Remove from oven; cool on wire racks. To preserve the crisp crust, do not store in plastic wrap or bags. Bread can be loosely covered or left out for up to two days before it dries out completely.

Note: Replace the 1 cup starter used by adding 1 cup warm (90–100°F.) milk and 1 cup flour to the pot. (Do the same for the ¾ cup starter: add ¾ cup warm milk and ¾ cup flour.) Let it stand in a warm (70–100°F.) place until bubbly, sour smelling, and a clear liquid has formed on top, about 12 to 24 hours. Stir, cover loosely, and refrigerate.

MENU SELECTION: DOUGH

WHOLE-GRAIN BREADS

✦✦ BASIC WHOLE WHEAT BREAD ✦✦

Like the Basic White Bread recipe, this is a simple, easy-to-make whole wheat bread. Keep a sliced loaf in your freezer and you'll always have a healthy bread on hand for sandwiches.

1½-POUND LOAF

½ cup water (for Welbilt/Dak
machines add 2 tablespoons
more water)
⅜ cup milk
1 egg
1½ cups whole wheat flour
1½ cups bread flour
1½ teaspoons salt
1½ tablespoons oil
1½ tablespoons honey
2 teaspoons Red Star brand
active dry yeast for all
machines

1-POUND LOAF

¼ cup water (for Welbilt
machine, no extra water
needed)
⅜ cup milk
1 egg
1 cup whole wheat flour
1 cup bread flour
1 teaspoon salt
1 tablespoon oil
1 tablespoon honey
2 teaspoons Red Star brand
active dry yeast for all
machines

Place all ingredients in bread pan, select Light Crust setting, and press Start.

After the baking cycle ends, remove bread from pan, place on cake rack, and allow to cool 1 hour before slicing.

> CRUST: LIGHT
> MENU SELECTION: BAKE (LIGHT)

⋆⋆ HEAVENLY WHOLE ⋆⋆
WHEAT BREAD

We think this is the best of our whole wheat breads. It's moist, has a good crust, and a flavor that's out of this world.

1½-POUND LOAF

1⅛ cups water (for Welbilt/Dak
machines add 2 tablespoons
more water)
2 cups whole wheat flour
1 cup bread flour
1½ teaspoons salt
4 tablespoons butter or
margarine
2 tablespoons sugar
¼ cup instant potato flakes
1½ teaspoons Red Star brand
active dry yeast for all
machines except 1½-pound
Welbilt/Dak machines (use 2
teaspoons yeast)

1-POUND LOAF

¾ cup water (for Welbilt
machine add 1 tablespoon
more water)
1⅓ cups whole wheat flour
⅔ cup bread flour
1 teaspoon salt
3 tablespoons butter or
margarine
1 tablespoon sugar
3 tablespoons instant potato
flakes
1½ teaspoons Red Star brand
active dry yeast for all
machines

Place all ingredients in bread pan, select Light Crust setting, and press Start.

After the baking cycle ends, remove bread from pan, place on cake rack, and allow to cool 1 hour before slicing.

> CRUST: LIGHT
> MENU SELECTION: BAKE (LIGHT)

** DEBBIE'S HONEY WHOLE ** WHEAT BREAD

This bread took some doing to perfect, but it was well worth the effort. It's a beautiful loaf with an exceptional texture and a sweet taste. Linda's sister Debbie loves serving this one to company. She says it's too sweet as a sandwich bread but it is marvelous plain or toasted with butter. (Note: In all machines except the Panasonic/National, the 1½-pound loaf can be made with 3 cups whole wheat flour; omit the bread flour.)

1½-POUND LOAF
1⅛ cups milk (for Welbilt/Dak
 machines add 3 tablespoons
 more milk)
2½ cups whole wheat flour
½ cup bread flour
½ teaspoon salt
1 tablespoon butter or
 margarine
¼ cup honey
2 teaspoons Red Star brand
 active dry yeast for all
 machines

1-POUND LOAF
¾ cup milk (for Welbilt machine
 add 1 tablespoon more milk)
2 cups whole wheat flour
¼ cup bread flour
½ teaspoon salt
2 teaspoons butter or margarine
3 tablespoons honey
2 teaspoons Red Star brand
 active dry yeast for all
 machines

Place all ingredients in bread pan, select Light Crust setting, and press Start.

After the baking cycle ends, remove bread from pan, place on cake rack, and allow to cool 1 hour before slicing.

```
CRUST: LIGHT
MENU SELECTION: BAKE (LIGHT)
```

·· MADELEINE'S NEIGHBORLY ··
BREAD

Our friend Madeleine loves this nicely shaped whole wheat potato bread. It's moist and wheaty, makes a lovely sandwich, and is a favorite of all the neighbors.

1½-POUND LOAF	1-POUND LOAF
⅝ cup milk	⅜ cup milk
⅜ cup potato water* (for Welbilt/Dak machines add 2 tablespoons more water)	¼ cup potato water* (for Welbilt machine add 1 tablespoon more water)
2 cups whole wheat flour	1⅓ cups whole wheat flour
1 cup bread flour	⅔ cup bread flour
⅓ cup plain mashed potato, at room temperature	¼ cup plain mashed potato, at room temperature
1½ teaspoons salt	1 teaspoon salt
1½ tablespoons butter or margarine	1 tablespoon butter or margarine
1½ tablespoons honey	1 tablespoon honey
2 teaspoons Red Star brand active dry yeast for all machines	2 teaspoons Red Star brand active dry yeast for all machines

Place all ingredients in bread pan, select Light Crust setting, and press Start.

After the baking cycle ends, remove bread from pan, place on cake rack, and allow to cool 1 hour before slicing.

> CRUST: LIGHT
> MENU SELECTION: BAKE (LIGHT)

---

*The water in which you cooked the potato.

** SAN DIEGO SUNSHINE BREAD **

Just like our hometown, this bread will delight your senses! It's a sweet whole wheat loaf with a delicate hint of orange. Pack up a picnic basket with a thermos of hot coffee or tea, a loaf of this bread, and some honey butter. Locate a city park or a sunny terrace and you'll have the makings for a romantic, leisurely breakfast.

1½-POUND LOAF	1-POUND LOAF
1 cup water (for Welbilt/Dak machines add 1 tablespoon more water)	¾ cup water (for Welbilt machine add 1 tablespoon more water)
2 cups bread flour	1⅓ cups bread flour
1 cup whole wheat flour	⅔ cup whole wheat flour
1 teaspoon salt	1 teaspoon salt
2 tablespoons butter or margarine	1½ tablespoons butter or margarine
2 tablespoons brown sugar	1 tablespoon brown sugar
2 tablespoons honey	1 tablespoon honey
Grated rind of 1½ oranges	Grated rind of 1 orange
1½ teaspoons Red Star brand active dry yeast for all machines except 1½-pound Welbilt/Dak machines (use 2 teaspoons yeast)	1½ teaspoons Red Star brand active dry yeast for all machines

Place all ingredients in bread pan, select Light Crust setting, and press Start.

After the baking cycle ends, remove bread from pan, place on cake rack, and allow to cool 1 hour before slicing.

```
CRUST: LIGHT
MENU SELECTION: BAKE (LIGHT)
```

•• APPLE-BUTTER WHEAT •• BREAD

Here's a good, mild, apple- and wheat-flavored breakfast toast. This is a very soft bread when it first comes out of the pan, so it's best to wait several hours before slicing it.

1½-POUND LOAF	1-POUND LOAF
1 cup water (for Welbilt/Dak machines add 1 tablespoon more water)	⅝ cup water (for Welbilt machine add 1 tablespoon more water)
1½ cups all-purpose flour	1 cup all-purpose flour
1½ cups whole wheat flour	1 cup whole wheat flour
1½ teaspoons salt	1 teaspoon salt
2 tablespoons butter or margarine	1 tablespoon butter or margarine
¼ cup apple butter	3 tablespoons apple butter
1½ teaspoons Red Star brand active dry yeast for all machines except 1½-pound Welbilt/Dak machines (use 2 teaspoons yeast)	1½ teaspoons Red Star brand active dry yeast for all machines

Place all ingredients in bread pan, select Light Crust setting, and press Start.

After the baking cycle ends, remove bread from pan, place on cake rack, and allow to cool at least 1 hour before slicing.

```
CRUST: LIGHT
MENU SELECTION: BAKE (LIGHT)
```

·· DAILY BREAD ··

Want a wholesome, high-fiber bread for an afternoon snack? Try this excellent, hearty loaf. It's a very tightly crumbed bread because it contains no white flour and it doesn't rise so high as most loaves.

1½-POUND LOAF

¼ cup miller's bran
⅜ cup milk
½ cup water (for Welbilt/Dak machines add 2 tablespoons more water)
1 egg
3 cups whole wheat flour
1½ teaspoons salt
1½ tablespoons butter or margarine
¼ cup honey
⅓ cup raw, unsalted sunflower seeds
2 teaspoons Red Star brand active dry yeast for all machines

1-POUND LOAF

3 tablespoons miller's bran
¼ cup milk
⅜ cup water (for Welbilt machine add 1 tablespoon more water)
1 egg
2 cups whole wheat flour
1 teaspoon salt
1 tablespoon butter or margarine
3 tablespoons honey
¼ cup raw, unsalted sunflower seeds
2 teaspoons Red Star brand active dry yeast for all machines

Place all ingredients in bread pan, select Light Crust setting, and press Start.

After the baking cycle ends, remove bread from pan, place on cake rack, and allow to cool 1 hour before slicing.

CRUST: LIGHT
MENU SELECTION: BAKE (LIGHT)

✦✦ WHOLE WHEAT SUNFLOWER ✦✦
BREAD

This bread is simply bursting with good things to eat, like oats, whole wheat flour, wheat germ, and sunflower seeds. The refreshing hint of orange blends beautifully with all that goodness. Use it for toast, sandwiches, or just plain snacking.

1½-POUND LOAF	1-POUND LOAF
½ cup old-fashioned rolled oats	⅓ cup old-fashioned rolled oats
1⅛ cups buttermilk (or 5 tablespoons dry buttermilk powder and 1⅛ cups water) (for Welbilt/Dak machines add 2 tablespoons more buttermilk)	⅝ cup buttermilk (or 3 tablespoons dry buttermilk powder and ⅝ cup water) (for Welbilt machine add 1 tablespoon more buttermilk)
1 egg	1 egg
1½ cups whole wheat flour	1 cup whole wheat flour
1½ cups bread flour	1 cup bread flour
1 tablespoon wheat germ	2 teaspoons wheat germ
1½ teaspoons salt	1 teaspoon salt
1½ tablespoons butter or margarine	1 tablespoon butter or margarine
2 tablespoons brown sugar	1 tablespoon brown sugar
Grated rind of 1½ oranges	Grated rind of 1 orange
⅓ cup raw, unsalted sunflower seeds	¼ cup raw, unsalted sunflower seeds
¼ teaspoon baking soda	¼ teaspoon baking soda
3 teaspoons Red Star brand active dry yeast for all machines	3 teaspoons Red Star brand active dry yeast for all machines

Place all ingredients in bread pan, select Light Crust setting, and press Start.

After the baking cycle ends, remove bread from pan, place on cake rack, and allow to cool 1 hour before slicing.

```
CRUST: LIGHT
MENU SELECTION: BAKE (LIGHT)
```

⋆⋆ SHREDDED-WHEAT BREAD ⋆⋆

When your mother told you to eat your shredded wheat, she never imagined it could be served up like this! This is a fine and flavorsome loaf of bread. (Note that the 1-pound loaf is baked on the Rapid Bake setting to prevent it from collapsing.)

1½-POUND LOAF

2 large shredded-wheat biscuits, crumbled

1⅛ cups water (for Welbilt/Dak machines add 2 tablespoons more water)

3 cups whole wheat flour

1½ teaspoons salt

1½ tablespoons butter or margarine

2 tablespoons brown sugar

2 tablespoons honey

2 teaspoons Red Star brand active dry yeast for all machines

1-POUND LOAF

1 large shredded-wheat biscuit, crumbled

⅞ cup water (for Welbilt machine add 1 tablespoon more water)

2 cups whole wheat flour

1 teaspoon salt

1 tablespoon butter or margarine

1½ tablespoons brown sugar

1½ tablespoons honey

2 teaspoons Red Star brand active dry yeast for all machines

FOR 1½-POUND LOAF

Place all ingredients in bread pan, select Light Crust setting, and press Start.

After the baking cycle ends, remove bread from pan, place on cake rack, and allow to cool 1 hour before slicing.

```
CRUST: LIGHT
MENU SELECTION: BAKE (LIGHT)
```

FOR 1-POUND LOAF

Place all ingredients in bread pan, select Rapid Bake setting, and press Start.

After the baking cycle ends, remove bread from pan, place on cake rack, and allow to cool 1 hour before slicing.

```
CRUST: REGULAR
MENU SELECTION: RAPID BAKE
```

◆◆ LOU'S BEER BREAD ◆◆

This one was contributed by a good friend who knows just about everything there is to know about beer. It's a moist, evenly textured bread that's good enough to eat plain. Cheers! (Note that the 1-pound Panasonic/National loaf needs to bake on Rapid Bake to prevent collapse. Also, to produce a nicer looking loaf in the 1½-pound Panasonic/National, reduce the milk to ¼ cup.)

1½-POUND LOAF

½ cup milk (for the Panasonic/
National, use ¼ cup milk)
1 cup flat bock beer (or any
dark beer) (for Welbilt/Dak
machines add 2 tablespoons
more beer)
3 cups whole wheat flour
3 tablespoons wheat germ
1 teaspoon salt
4 tablespoons butter or
margarine
1½ tablespoons molasses
1½ tablespoons honey
2 teaspoons Red Star brand
active dry yeast for all
machines

1-POUND LOAF

¼ cup milk
⅝ cup flat bock beer (or any
dark beer) (for Welbilt
machine add 1 tablespoon
more beer)
2 cups whole wheat flour
2 tablespoons wheat germ
½ teaspoon salt
3 tablespoons butter or
margarine
1 tablespoon molasses
1 tablespoon honey
2 teaspoons Red Star brand
active dry yeast for all
machines

FOR 1½-POUND LOAF

Place all ingredients in bread pan, select Light Crust setting, and press Start.

After the baking cycle ends, remove bread from pan, place on cake rack, and allow to cool 1 hour before slicing.

```
CRUST: LIGHT
MENU SELECTION: BAKE (LIGHT)
```

FOR 1-POUND LOAF

Place all ingredients in bread pan, select Rapid Bake setting, and press Start.

After the baking cycle ends, remove bread from pan, place on cake rack, and allow to cool 1 hour before slicing.

```
CRUST: REGULAR
MENU SELECTION: RAPID BAKE
```

✦✦ MILLER'S BRAN BREAD ✦✦

If you're looking for a good sandwich bread, try this soft, light bran bread. It's a nice change from the stronger whole wheat taste, yet is still nutritious.

1½-POUND LOAF
½ cup miller's bran
¾ cup + 1 tablespoon water
  (for Welbilt/Dak machines add
  no extra water)
1 egg
2½ cups bread flour
1½ teaspoons salt
1½ tablespoons oil
1½ tablespoons honey
1½ teaspoons Red Star brand
  active dry yeast for all
  machines except 1½-pound
  Welbilt/Dak machines (use 2
  teaspoons yeast)

1-POUND LOAF
⅓ cup miller's bran
⅝ cup water (for Welbilt
  machine add no extra water)
1 egg
1⅔ cups bread flour
1 teaspoon salt
1 tablespoon oil
1 tablespoon honey
1½ teaspoons Red Star brand
  active dry yeast for all
  machines

Place all ingredients in bread pan, select Light Crust setting, and press Start.

After the baking cycle ends, remove bread from pan, place on cake rack, and allow to cool 1 hour before slicing.

```
CRUST: LIGHT
MENU SELECTION: BAKE (LIGHT)
```

◆◆ CRACKED-WHEAT BREAD ◆◆

Don't overlook the first step on this bread; it's important to cook the cracked wheat to soften it. This recipe requires a few extra minutes preparation time, but you'll be pleased with the results.

1½-POUND LOAF
¾ cup water
⅓ cup cracked wheat
¾ cup milk (for Welbilt/Dak machines add 2 tablespoons more water)
2¼ cups bread flour
¾ cup whole wheat flour
1½ teaspoons salt
2 tablespoons butter or margarine
1½ tablespoons honey
1½ tablespoons molasses
2 teaspoons Red Star brand active dry yeast for all machines

1-POUND LOAF
½ cup water
¼ cup cracked wheat
½ cup milk (for Welbilt machine add 1 tablespoon more water)
1½ cups bread flour
½ cup whole wheat flour
1 teaspoon salt
1½ tablespoons butter or margarine
1 tablespoon honey
1 tablespoon molasses
2 teaspoons Red Star brand active dry yeast for all machines

In a small saucepan, heat the water to boiling; add cracked wheat. Cook on medium-high heat for approximately 6 minutes until all the water is absorbed; stir occasionally with a wooden spoon. Remove pan from heat; allow cracked wheat to cool to room temperature.

Place all ingredients, including cooled cracked wheat, in bread pan and press Start.

After the baking cycle ends, remove bread from pan, place on cake rack, and allow to cool 1 hour before slicing.

CRUST: REGULAR
MENU SELECTION: BAKE

◆◆ BUTTERMILK CRACKED-WHEAT ◆◆ BREAD

The raw cracked wheat adds a crunchy texture to this noteworthy whole wheat bread. It's not as tall as some loaves, but it's just as delicious. Serve it proudly with dinner or use it for sandwiches.

1½-POUND LOAF

½ cup cracked wheat
1⅜ cups buttermilk (or 5 tablespoons dry buttermilk powder and 1⅜ cups water) (for Welbilt/Dak machines add 2 tablespoons more buttermilk)
2 cups whole wheat flour
1 cup bread flour
1½ teaspoons salt
1 tablespoon shortening
2 tablespoons honey
¼ teaspoon baking soda
2 teaspoons Red Star brand active dry yeast for all machines

1-POUND LOAF

⅓ cup cracked wheat
⅞ cup buttermilk (or 3 tablespoons dry buttermilk powder and ⅞ cup water) (for Welbilt machine add 1 tablespoon more buttermilk)
1⅓ cups whole wheat flour
⅔ cup bread flour
1 teaspoon salt
1 tablespoon shortening
1½ tablespoons honey
¼ teaspoon baking soda
2 teaspoons Red Star brand active dry yeast for all machines

Place all ingredients in bread pan, select Light Crust setting, and press Start.

After the baking cycle ends, remove bread from pan, place on cake rack, and allow to cool 1 hour before slicing.

```
CRUST: LIGHT
MENU SELECTION: BAKE (LIGHT)
```

❖❖ BULGUR WHEAT BREAD ❖❖

Healthy never tasted so good! Try this superb bread while it's still slightly warm for the most intense whole-grain flavor.

1½-POUND LOAF	1-POUND LOAF
½ cup water	½ cup water
⅓ cup bulgur wheat	¼ cup bulgur wheat
½ cup old-fashioned rolled oats	¼ cup old-fashioned rolled oats
1⅛ cups water (for Welbilt/Dak machines add 2 tablespoons more water)	⅞ cup water (for Welbilt machine add 1 tablespoon more water)
1½ cups bread flour	1 cup bread flour
1½ cups whole wheat flour	1 cup whole wheat flour
2 tablespoons cornmeal	1 tablespoon cornmeal
1½ teaspoons salt	1 teaspoon salt
2 tablespoons butter or margarine	1 tablespoon butter or margarine
1 tablespoon molasses	2 teaspoons molasses
1 tablespoon honey	2 teaspoons honey
2 teaspoons Red Star brand active dry yeast for all machines	2 teaspoons Red Star brand active dry yeast for all machines

In a small saucepan, heat water to boiling; add bulgur. Cook on medium-high heat for approximately 5 to 6 minutes until all the water is absorbed; stir occasionally with a wooden spoon. Remove pan from heat; allow bulgur to cool to room temperature.

Place all ingredients in bread pan and press Start.

After the baking cycle ends, remove bread from pan, place on cake rack, and allow to cool 30 minutes before slicing.

> CRUST: REGULAR
> MENU SELECTION: BAKE

•• LOIS'S RYE BREAD ••

Lois's favorite bread is this densely textured basic rye bread. It has a great crust and is reminiscent of a good Jewish rye. Toasted or used for a sandwich, it's delicious.

1½-POUND LOAF	1-POUND LOAF
⅝ cup milk	½ cup milk
¾ cup water (for Welbilt/Dak machines add 3 tablespoons more water)	⅜ cup water (for Welbilt machine add 1 tablespoon more water)
1½ cups whole wheat flour	1 cup whole wheat flour
1½ cups bread flour	1 cup bread flour
1 cup rye flour	½ cup rye flour
1½ teaspoons salt	1 teaspoon salt
1½ tablespoons butter or margarine	1 tablespoon butter or margarine
3 tablespoons molasses	2 tablespoons molasses
1 tablespoon caraway seeds	2 teaspoons caraway seeds
2 teaspoons Red Star brand active dry yeast for all machines	2 teaspoons Red Star brand active dry yeast for all machines

Place all ingredients in bread pan and press Start.

After the baking cycle ends, remove bread from pan, place on cake rack, and allow to cool 1 hour before slicing.

CRUST: REGULAR
MENU SELECTION: BAKE

✦✦ LORRAINE'S BUTTERMILK ✦✦
RYE BREAD

A good friend, and our favorite critic, Lorraine loved every loaf she sampled. She selected this as one of her favorites. We agree. With its creamy texture and rich flavor, it's perfect for sandwiches.

1½-POUND LOAF	1-POUND LOAF
1⅜ cups buttermilk (or 5 tablespoons dry buttermilk powder and 1⅜ cup water) (for Welbilt/Dak machines add 3 tablespoons more buttermilk)	⅞ cup buttermilk (or 3 tablespoons dry buttermilk powder and ⅞ cup water) (for Welbilt machine add 1 tablespoon more buttermilk)
3 cups bread flour	2 cups bread flour
1 cup rye flour	⅓ cup rye flour
1½ teaspoons salt	1 teaspoon salt
1½ tablespoons butter or margarine	1 tablespoon butter or margarine
2 tablespoons brown sugar	1½ tablespoons brown sugar
¼ teaspoon baking soda	¼ teaspoon baking soda
1 teaspoon caraway seeds	1 teaspoon caraway seeds
3 teaspoons Red Star brand active dry yeast for all machines	2 teaspoons Red Star brand active dry yeast for all machines

Place all ingredients in bread pan, select Light Crust setting, and press Start.

After the baking cycle ends, remove bread from pan, place on cake rack, and allow to cool 1 hour before slicing.

```
CRUST: LIGHT
MENU SELECTION: BAKE (LIGHT)
```

◆◆ CHEDDAR RYE BREAD ◆◆

Because this loaf doesn't rise exceptionally high, it has a very dense texture. Slice it thin and spread with chopped liver or a pâté for exceptional hors d'oeuvre. We've also found that it doesn't keep well; after a day or two, the crust hardens. Use it for hors d'oeuvre the first day or as a doorstop the third day.

1½-POUND LOAF	1-POUND LOAF
⅝ cup buttermilk	⅜ cup buttermilk
½ cup water (for Welbilt/Dak machines add 3 tablespoons more water)	⅜ cup water (for Welbilt machine add 1 tablespoon more water)
2½ cups bread flour	1⅔ cups bread flour
1 cup rye flour	⅔ cup rye flour
1 teaspoon salt	¾ teaspoon salt
1½ teaspoons oil	1 teaspoon oil
1½ tablespoons light brown sugar	1 tablespoon light brown sugar
1 cup (4 ounces) grated sharp Cheddar cheese	½ cup (2 ounces) grated sharp Cheddar cheese
1 tablespoon caraway seeds (optional)	2 teaspoons caraway seeds (optional)
3 teaspoons Red Star brand active dry yeast for all machines	2 teaspoons Red Star brand active dry yeast for all machines

Place all ingredients in bread pan, select Light Crust setting, and press Start.

After the baking cycle ends, remove bread from pan, place on cake rack, and allow to cool 1 hour before slicing.

```
CRUST: LIGHT
MENU SELECTION: BAKE (LIGHT)
```

49

∗∗ HIS FAVORITE RYE BREAD ∗∗

This is a small, well-shaped loaf with a robust, yeasty, and slightly sweet taste. Half a bottle of beer goes into this loaf; the other half goes to the nearest man. So if you ask, he'll probably tell you this is his favorite rye bread.

1½-POUND LOAF	1-POUND LOAF
¾ cup flat beer	⅝ cup flat beer
⅜ cup water (for Welbilt/Dak machines add 1 tablespoon more water)	¼ cup water (for Welbilt machine add 1 tablespoon more water)
2½ cups bread flour	1½ cups bread flour
1 cup rye flour	¾ cup rye flour
½ teaspoon salt	½ teaspoon salt
1½ tablespoons shortening	1 tablespoon shortening
2 tablespoons brown sugar	1½ tablespoons brown sugar
2 tablespoons molasses	1½ tablespoons molasses
Grated rind of 1 orange (optional)	Grated rind of ½ orange (optional)
2 teaspoons caraway seeds	1 teaspoon caraway seeds
3 teaspoons Red Star brand active dry yeast for all machines	2 teaspoons Red Star brand active dry yeast for all machines

Place all ingredients in bread pan, select Light Crust setting, and press Start.

After the baking cycle ends, remove bread from pan, place on cake rack, and allow to cool 1 hour before slicing.

```
CRUST: LIGHT
MENU SELECTION: BAKE (LIGHT)
```

◆◆ MICHAEL'S ONION RYE ◆◆

When Lois's son Michael comes to visit, she bakes this bread for him. It has a very welcoming aroma. Serve this tasty rye slightly warm to enjoy it at its best.

<table>
<tr><td colspan="2" align="center">1½-POUND LOAF</td><td colspan="2" align="center">1-POUND LOAF</td></tr>
</table>

1½-POUND LOAF

1⅛ cups water (for Welbilt/Dak machines add 2 tablespoons more water)
1½ cups whole wheat flour
1½ cups bread flour
¾ cup rye flour
1½ teaspoons salt
1 tablespoon oil
1 tablespoon molasses
⅓ cup minced onion
1 teaspoon caraway seeds
2 teaspoons Red Star brand active dry yeast for all machines

1-POUND LOAF

¾ cup + 1 tablespoon water (for Welbilt machine add 1 tablespoon more water)
1 cup whole wheat flour
1 cup bread flour
½ cup rye flour
1 teaspoon salt
2 teaspoons oil
2 teaspoons molasses
¼ cup minced onion
1 teaspoon caraway seeds
2 teaspoons Red Star brand active dry yeast for all machines

Place all ingredients in bread pan and press Start.

After the baking cycle ends, remove bread from pan, place on cake rack, and allow to cool 30 minutes before slicing.

```
CRUST: REGULAR
MENU SELECTION: BAKE
```

⬩⬩ CITRUS RYE ⬩⬩

There's a delicate citrus flavor in this aromatic rye bread. It makes superb croutons for a Caesar salad.

1½-POUND LOAF

⅝ cup milk
½ cup water (for Welbilt/Dak
   machines add 2 tablespoons
   more water)
2½ cups bread flour
1 cup rye flour
1½ teaspoons salt
2 tablespoons shortening
2 tablespoons molasses
2 tablespoons brown sugar
Grated rind of ½ orange
Grated rind of ½ lemon
1 tablespoon caraway seeds
   (optional)
2 teaspoons Red Star brand
   active dry yeast for all
   machines

1-POUND LOAF

½ cup milk
⅜ cup water (for Welbilt
   machine add 1 tablespoon
   more water)
2 cups bread flour
½ cup rye flour
1 teaspoon salt
1½ tablespoons shortening
1 tablespoon molasses
1 tablespoon brown sugar
Grated rind of ½ orange
Grated rind of ½ lemon
2 teaspoons caraway seeds
   (optional)
2 teaspoons Red Star brand
   active dry yeast for all
   machines

Place all ingredients in bread pan, select Light Crust setting, and press Start.

After the baking cycle ends, remove bread from pan, place on cake rack, and allow to cool 1 hour before slicing.

```
CRUST: LIGHT
MENU SELECTION: BAKE (LIGHT)
```

** SWEDISH LIMPA RYE BREAD **

The fennel seeds add an unusual licorice flavor to this bread. Thinly sliced, it's good enough for any smorgasbord.

1½-POUND LOAF	1-POUND LOAF
1⅛ cups water (for Welbilt/Dak machines add 2 tablespoons more water)	*¾ cup water (for Welbilt machine add 1 tablespoon more water)*
2½ cups bread flour	*1⅓ cups bread flour*
1 cup rye flour	*⅔ cup rye flour*
1 teaspoon salt	*½ teaspoon salt*
1 tablespoon oil	*2 teaspoons oil*
1 tablespoon honey	*2 teaspoons honey*
1 teaspoon caraway seeds	*½ teaspoon caraway seeds*
½ teaspoon fennel seeds	*¼ teaspoon fennel seeds*
Grated rind of 1½ oranges	*Grated rind of 1 orange*
1½ teaspoons Red Star brand active dry yeast for all machines except 1½-pound Welbilt/Dak machines (use 2 teaspoons yeast)	*1½ teaspoons Red Star brand active dry yeast for all machines*

Place all ingredients in bread pan and press Start.

After the baking cycle ends, remove bread from pan, place on cake rack, and allow to cool 1 hour before slicing.

CRUST: REGULAR
MENU SELECTION: BAKE

•• SAUERKRAUT RYE BREAD ••

Talk about a hearty bread . . . here's one that's almost a meal in itself! It's moist, soft, and has the unmistakable flavor of sauerkraut. A slice of this bread would be a great accompaniment to steaming hot vegetable soup on a chilly winter night. It would also taste wonderful with thin slices of corned beef, Swiss cheese, and a sweet, hot mustard.

1½-POUND LOAF

¾ cup water (for Welbilt/Dak machines add 2 tablespoons more water)

2 cups bread flour

1 cup rye flour

1½ teaspoons salt

1½ tablespoons brown sugar

1½ tablespoons molasses

1½ tablespoons butter or margarine

1 cup sauerkraut, squeezed, well drained, and chopped

1 tablespoon caraway seeds

1½ teaspoons Red Star brand active dry yeast for all machines except 1½-pound Welbilt/Dak machines (use 2 teaspoons yeast)

1-POUND LOAF

½ cup water (for Welbilt machine no extra water is needed)

1⅓ cups bread flour

⅔ cup rye flour

1 teaspoon salt

1 tablespoon brown sugar

1 tablespoon molasses

1 tablespoon butter or margarine

½ cup sauerkraut, squeezed, well drained, and chopped

2 teaspoons caraway seeds

2 teaspoons Red Star brand active dry yeast for all machines

Place all ingredients in bread pan, select Light Crust setting, and press Start.

After the baking cycle ends, remove bread from pan, place on cake rack, and allow to cool 1 hour before slicing.

```
CRUST: LIGHT
MENU SELECTION: BAKE (LIGHT)
```

•• DILLY DELI RYE ••

This will be a taste sensation at dinner; your guests will rave! It's a rye bread with the unmistakable flavor of pickles.

1½-POUND LOAF	1-POUND LOAF
⅝ cup water (for Welbilt/Dak machines add 2 tablespoons more water)	⅜ cup water (for Welbilt machine add 1 tablespoon more water)
⅜ cup brine from dill pickles	¼ cup brine from dill pickles
1 egg	1 egg
2 cups bread flour	1⅓ cups bread flour
1 cup rye flour	⅔ cup rye flour
1 teaspoon salt	¾ teaspoon salt
1½ tablespoons oil	1 tablespoon oil
2 tablespoons sugar	1½ tablespoons sugar
1½ teaspoons dried dill	1 teaspoon dried dill
2 teaspoons Red Star brand active dry yeast for all machines	2 teaspoons Red Star brand active dry yeast for all machines

Place all ingredients in bread pan, select Light Crust setting, and press Start.

After the baking cycle ends, remove bread from pan, place on cake rack, and allow to cool 1 hour before slicing.

CRUST: LIGHT
MENU SELECTION: BAKE (LIGHT)

❖❖ VOLLKORNBROT ❖❖

We almost tossed this recipe out, because it consistently resulted in oddly shaped loaves. But the flavor of this stout-hearted bread so closely resembled some of the wonderful breads we'd eaten in Germany that it would have been a crime to omit it. Just be forewarned—it's a funny-looking bread with a flavor and personality all its own. You haven't lived until you've tried this one with a hunk of cheese. *Wunderbar!*

1½-POUND LOAF	1-POUND LOAF
1½ cups buttermilk (or 6 tablespoons dry buttermilk powder and 1½ cups water) (for Welbilt/Dak machines add 2 tablespoons more buttermilk)	*⅞ cup buttermilk (or 3 tablespoons dry buttermilk powder and ⅞ cup water) (for Welbilt machine add 1 tablespoon more buttermilk)*
	3 tablespoons water
2½ cups whole wheat flour	*1 cup whole wheat flour*
½ cup bread flour	*1 cup bread flour*
½ cup rye flour	*2 tablespoons rye flour*
¼ cup buckwheat flour	*2 tablespoons buckwheat flour*
¼ cup wheat germ	*2 tablespoons wheat germ*
1 teaspoon salt	*½ teaspoon salt*
1 tablespoon butter or margarine	*1 tablespoon butter or margarine*
¼ cup molasses	*2 tablespoons molasses*
3 teaspoons Red Star brand active dry yeast for all machines	*3 teaspoons Red Star brand active dry yeast for all machines*

Place all ingredients in bread pan, select Light Crust setting, and press Start.

After the baking cycle ends, remove bread from pan, place on cake rack, and allow to cool 1 hour before slicing.

```
CRUST: LIGHT
MENU SELECTION: BAKE (LIGHT)
```

** BLACK FOREST **
PUMPERNICKEL

This is a dark bread with that fabulous, distinctive rye flavor. Pair this soul-satisfying bread with thin slices of ham and cheese or a mug of homemade potato soup.

1½-POUND LOAF

1⅛ cups water (for Welbilt/Dak
   machines add 2 tablespoons
   more water)
1½ cups bread flour
1 cup rye flour
1 cup whole wheat flour
1½ teaspoons salt
1½ tablespoons oil
⅓ cup molasses
3 tablespoons cocoa powder
1 tablespoon caraway seeds
2 teaspoons Red Star brand
   active dry yeast for all
   machines

1-POUND LOAF

¾ cup water (for Welbilt
   machine add 1 tablespoon
   more water)
⅔ cup bread flour
⅔ cup rye flour
⅔ cup whole wheat flour
1 teaspoon salt
1 tablespoon oil
3 tablespoons molasses
2 tablespoons cocoa powder
2 teaspoons caraway seeds
2 teaspoons Red Star brand
   active dry yeast for all
   machines

Place all ingredients in bread pan, select Light Crust setting, and press Start.

After the baking cycle ends, remove bread from pan, place on cake rack, and allow to cool 1 hour before slicing.

```
CRUST: LIGHT
MENU SELECTION: BAKE (LIGHT)
```

·· MORRIS AND EVELYN'S OLD ··
WORLD PUMPERNICKEL

Because it has a bumpy top, this pumpernickel may not be the best looking of breads, but its flavor can't be beat! Its pleasant, tangy taste is enhanced by the moist texture of the potato. This bread is named for Lois's parents because they adore Old World breads such as this one.

1½-POUND LOAF	1-POUND LOAF
2 tablespoons miller's bran	*1 tablespoon miller's bran*
1 cup potato water,* cooled (for Welbilt/Dak machines add 2 tablespoons more water)	*¾ cup potato water,* cooled (for Welbilt machine add 1 tablespoon more water)*
3 cups whole wheat flour	*2 cups whole wheat flour*
½ cup rye flour	*⅓ cup rye flour*
2 tablespoons cornmeal	*1 tablespoon cornmeal*
½ cup plain mashed potato, at room temperature	*¼ cup plain mashed potato, at room temperature*
1½ teaspoons salt	*1 teaspoon salt*
1½ tablespoons butter or margarine	*1 tablespoon butter or margarine*
1½ tablespoons molasses	*1 tablespoon molasses*
1 teaspoon caraway seeds	*½ teaspoon caraway seeds*
3 teaspoons Red Star brand active dry yeast for all machines	*2 teaspoons Red Star brand active dry yeast for all machines*

Place all ingredients in bread pan and press Start.

After the baking cycle ends, remove bread from pan, place on cake rack, and allow to cool 1 hour before slicing.

```
CRUST: REGULAR
MENU SELECTION: BAKE
```

*The water in which you cooked the potato.

◆◆ FARMHOUSE PUMPERNICKEL ◆◆

We love this chocolate-brown, robust pumpernickel with its sweet taste of molasses and raisins. On a cold winter night, cozy up in front of the fireplace with a slice of this bread, a steaming mug of your favorite soup, and a good book.

1½-POUND LOAF

1 cup water (for Welbilt/Dak
  machines add 2 tablespoons
  more water)
1 egg
2½ cups bread flour
1 cup rye flour
1 teaspoon salt
2 tablespoons shortening
3 tablespoons molasses
2½ tablespoons cocoa powder
1 tablespoon caraway seeds
¼ cup raisins
2 teaspoons Red Star brand
  active dry yeast for all
  machines

1-POUND LOAF

⅞ cup water (for Welbilt
  machine add 1 tablespoon
  more water)
1⅓ cups bread flour
⅔ cup rye flour
½ teaspoon salt
1 tablespoon shortening
2 tablespoons molasses
2 tablespoons cocoa powder
2 teaspoons caraway seeds
3 tablespoons raisins
2 teaspoons Red Star brand
  active dry yeast for all
  machines

Place all ingredients in bread pan and press Start.

After the baking cycle ends, remove bread from pan, place on cake rack, and allow to cool 1 hour before slicing.

CRUST: REGULAR
MENU SELECTION: BAKE

◆◆ RUSSIAN BLACK BREAD ◆◆

The vinegar in this lush, dark pumpernickel adds a bite to it. Try a slice of this unusually tall loaf of Slavic bread with an icy mug of German beer and some good Danish cheese for a glorious combination of international flavors.

1½-POUND LOAF

1⅛ cups water (no extra water
needed for Welbilt/Dak
machines)
2 tablespoons cider vinegar
2½ cups bread flour
1 cup rye flour
1 teaspoon salt
2 tablespoons butter or
margarine
2 tablespoons dark corn syrup
1 tablespoon brown sugar
3 tablespoons cocoa powder
1 teaspoon instant coffee
powder
1 tablespoon caraway seeds
¼ teaspoon fennel seeds
(optional)
2 teaspoons Red Star brand
active dry yeast for all
machines

1-POUND LOAF

⅞ cup water (no extra water
needed for Welbilt machine)
1½ tablespoons cider vinegar
2 cups bread flour
½ cup rye flour
1 teaspoon salt
1½ tablespoons butter or
margarine
1½ tablespoons dark corn syrup
2 teaspoons brown sugar
2 tablespoons cocoa powder
¾ teaspoon instant coffee
powder
2 teaspoons caraway seeds
Pinch of fennel seeds (optional)
2 teaspoons Red Star brand
active dry yeast for all
machines

Place all ingredients in bread pan and press Start.

After the baking cycle ends, remove bread from pan, place on cake rack, and allow to cool 1 hour before slicing.

```
CRUST: REGULAR
MENU SELECTION: BAKE
```

∙∙ RICK'S SEVEN-GRAIN BREAD ∙∙

Seven-grain cereal can usually be found in health-food stores, if not at your local market. This bread smells lovely baking, rises beautifully, and has a slightly crunchy texture. It's great for munching on in the wee small hours of the morning when only computer wizards, like Linda's brother-in-law Rick, are still awake.

1½-POUND LOAF	1-POUND LOAF
⅞ cup water (for Welbilt/Dak machines add 2 tablespoons more water)	⅝ cup water (for Welbilt machine no extra water is needed)
1 egg	1 egg
2½ cups whole wheat flour	1⅔ cups whole wheat flour
½ cup seven-grain cereal	⅓ cup seven-grain cereal
1½ teaspoons salt	1 teaspoon salt
2 tablespoons oil	1½ tablespoons oil
2 tablespoons honey	1½ tablespoons honey
2 teaspoons Red Star brand active dry yeast for all machines	2 teaspoons Red Star brand active dry yeast for all machines

Place all ingredients in bread pan, select Light Crust setting, and press Start.

After the baking cycle ends, remove bread from pan, place on cake rack, and allow to cool 1 hour before slicing.

```
CRUST: LIGHT
MENU SELECTION: BAKE (LIGHT)
```

•• MULTIGRAIN BUTTERMILK ••
BREAD

An earthy, wholesome-tasting bread, this makes sublime sandwiches.

1½-POUND LOAF

⅓ cup cracked wheat

1¼ cups buttermilk (or 5
   tablespoons dry buttermilk
   powder and 1¼ cups water)
   (for Welbilt/Dak machines add
   2 tablespoons more
   buttermilk)

1½ cups bread flour

1½ cups whole wheat flour

2 tablespoons wheat germ

¼ cup cornmeal

1½ teaspoons salt

1½ tablespoons butter or
   margarine

2 tablespoons honey

¼ teaspoon baking soda

3 teaspoons Red Star brand
   active dry yeast for all
   machines

1-POUND LOAF

¼ cup cracked wheat

⅞ cup buttermilk (or 3
   tablespoons dry buttermilk
   powder and ⅞ cup water)
   (for Welbilt machine add 1
   tablespoon more buttermilk)

1 cup bread flour

1 cup whole wheat flour

1½ tablespoons wheat germ

3 tablespoons cornmeal

1 teaspoon salt

1 tablespoon butter or
   margarine

1½ tablespoons honey

¼ teaspoon baking soda

2 teaspoons Red Star brand
   active dry yeast for all
   machines

Place all ingredients in bread pan, select Light Crust setting, and press Start.

After the baking cycle ends, remove bread from pan, place on cake rack, and allow to cool 1 hour before slicing.

CRUST: LIGHT
MENU SELECTION: BAKE (LIGHT)

✦✦ MARILYN'S EVERYDAY ✦✦
HEALTH BREAD

A create-your-own recipe, this is a good one for using up those odds and ends of various grains you may have on hand. Our friend Marilyn gave us this recipe. She owns a bread machine, too, and this is the only bread she makes!

1½-POUND LOAF	1-POUND LOAF
1¼ cups water (for Welbilt/Dak machines add 2 tablespoons more water)	⅞ cup water (for Welbilt machine add 1 tablespoon more water)
1½ cups whole wheat flour	1 cup whole wheat flour
1½ cups bread flour	1 cup bread flour
½ cup whole grains*	½ cup whole grains*
1½ teaspoons salt	1 teaspoon salt
1½ tablespoons butter or margarine	1 tablespoon butter or margarine
3 tablespoons sugar	2 tablespoons sugar
1½ tablespoons nonfat dry milk powder	1 tablespoon nonfat dry milk powder
2 teaspoons Red Star brand active dry yeast for all machines	2 teaspoons Red Star brand active dry yeast for all machines

Place all ingredients in bread pan, select Light Crust setting, and press Start.

After the baking cycle ends, remove bread from pan, place on cake rack, and allow to cool 1 hour before slicing.

> CRUST: LIGHT
> MENU SELECTION: BAKE (LIGHT)

*The ½ cup whole grains could be: ½ cup oats; ¼ cup oats and ¼ cup miller's bran; 2 tablespoons each miller's bran, oats, cracked wheat, and oat bran; or any amount of various grains to equal ½ cup.

⋄⋄ ZUNI INDIAN BREAD ⋄⋄

This is one of the first whole-grain breads we made in the bread machine. We've baked this nourishing bread many times since; it's definitely one of our favorites. We've also found it to be one of our most appreciated gift breads.

1½-POUND LOAF

⅞ cup buttermilk (or 3
  tablespoons dry buttermilk
  powder and ⅞ cup water)
  (for Welbilt/Dak machines add
  3 tablespoons more
  buttermilk)
1 egg
1⅔ cups whole wheat flour
1 cup bread flour
⅓ cup cornmeal
1½ teaspoons salt
1½ tablespoons butter or
  margarine
3 tablespoons molasses
⅓ cup raw, unsalted sunflower
  seeds
¼ teaspoon baking soda
3 teaspoons Red Star brand
  active dry yeast for all
  machines

1-POUND LOAF

⅝ cup buttermilk (or 2
  tablespoons dry buttermilk
  powder and ⅝ cup water)
  (for Welbilt machine add 1
  tablespoon more buttermilk)
1 egg
1 cup whole wheat flour
¾ cup bread flour
¼ cup cornmeal
1 teaspoon salt
1 tablespoon butter or
  margarine
2 tablespoons molasses
¼ cup raw, unsalted sunflower
  seeds
¼ teaspoon baking soda
3 teaspoons Red Star brand
  active dry yeast for all
  machines

Place all ingredients in bread pan, select Light Crust setting, and press Start.

After the baking cycle ends, remove bread from pan, place on cake rack, and allow to cool 1 hour before slicing.

```
CRUST: LIGHT
MENU SELECTION: BAKE (LIGHT)
```

•• BRISCOE'S IRISH ••
BROWN BREAD

The combination of caraway and raisins gives this healthy bread an unusual taste. We hope you like it as much as Briscoe does.

1½-POUND LOAF

⅓ cup old-fashioned rolled oats
1¼ cups buttermilk (or 5 tablespoons dry buttermilk powder and 1¼ cups water) (for Welbilt/Dak machines add 2 tablespoons more buttermilk)
2 cups whole wheat flour
1 cup bread flour
2 tablespoons oat bran
1 teaspoon salt
1½ tablespoons butter or margarine
3 tablespoons brown sugar
3 tablespoons raisins
1 tablespoon caraway seeds
¼ teaspoon baking soda
2 teaspoons Red Star brand active dry yeast for all machines

1-POUND LOAF

¼ cup old-fashioned rolled oats
1 cup buttermilk (or 4 tablespoons dry buttermilk powder and 1 cup water) (for Welbilt machine add 1 tablespoon more buttermilk)
1⅓ cups whole wheat flour
⅔ cup bread flour
1 tablespoon oat bran
1 teaspoon salt
1 tablespoon butter or margarine
2 tablespoons brown sugar
2 tablespoons raisins
2 teaspoons caraway seeds
¼ teaspoon baking soda
2 teaspoons Red Star brand active dry yeast for all machines

Place all ingredients in bread pan, select Light Crust setting, and press Start.

After the baking cycle ends, remove bread from pan, place on cake rack, and allow to cool 1 hour before slicing.

CRUST: LIGHT
MENU SELECTION: BAKE (LIGHT)

✻✻ WHOLE-WHEAT SODA BREAD ✻✻

Children love this rich-tasting soda bread. It's one that rose quite high in our machines.

1½-POUND LOAF

1¼ cups buttermilk (or 5
  tablespoons dry buttermilk
  powder and 1¼ cups water)
  (for Welbilt/Dak machines add
  2 tablespoons more
  buttermilk)
2 cups whole wheat flour
1 cup bread flour
1½ teaspoons salt
1½ tablespoons butter or
  margarine
1½ tablespoons honey
½ teaspoon baking soda
2 teaspoons Red Star brand
  active dry yeast for all
  machines

1-POUND LOAF

⅞ cup buttermilk (or 3
  tablespoons dry buttermilk
  powder and ⅞ cup water)
  (for Welbilt machine add 1
  tablespoon more buttermilk)
1⅓ cups whole wheat flour
⅔ cup bread flour
1 teaspoon salt
1 tablespoon butter or
  margarine
1 tablespoon honey
¼ teaspoon baking soda
2 teaspoons Red Star brand
  active dry yeast for all
  machines

Place all ingredients in bread pan, select Light Crust setting, and press Start.

After the baking cycle ends, remove bread from pan, place on cake rack, and allow to cool 1 hour before slicing.

CRUST: LIGHT
MENU SELECTION: BAKE (LIGHT)

✦✦ IRISH SODA BREAD ✦✦

Your friends will love you if you give them a loaf of this bread! It has a scrumptious old-country flavor.

1½-POUND LOAF

½ cup old-fashioned rolled oats
1¼ cups buttermilk (or 5
  tablespoons dry buttermilk
  powder and 1¼ cups water)
  (for Welbilt/Dak machines add
  3 tablespoons more
  buttermilk)
3 cups whole wheat flour
½ teaspoon baking soda
1 teaspoon salt
1½ tablespoons butter or
  margarine
3 tablespoons honey
⅓ cup raisins (optional)
3 teaspoons Red Star brand
  active dry yeast for all
  machines

1-POUND LOAF

⅓ cup old-fashioned rolled oats
⅞ cup buttermilk (or 3
  tablespoons dry buttermilk
  powder and ⅞ cup water)
  (for Welbilt machine add 1
  tablespoon more buttermilk)
2 cups whole wheat flour
½ teaspoon baking soda
1 teaspoon salt
1 tablespoon butter or
  margarine
2 tablespoons honey
¼ cup raisins (optional)
1½ teaspoons Red Star brand
  active dry yeast for all
  machines

Place all ingredients in bread pan, select Light Crust setting, and press Start.

After the baking cycle ends, remove bread from pan, place on cake rack, and allow to cool 1 hour before slicing.

```
CRUST: LIGHT
MENU SELECTION: BAKE (LIGHT)
```

•• HONEY 'N' OATS BREAD ••

The egg and oats lend a wonderful rich, creamy flavor to this bread. Serve it with a crock of sweet butter and homemade preserves.

1½-POUND LOAF

½ cup old-fashioned rolled oats
1 cup buttermilk (or 4
   tablespoons dry buttermilk
   powder and 1 cup water) (for
   Welbilt/Dak machines add 2
   tablespoons more buttermilk)
1 egg
1½ cups whole wheat flour
1½ cups bread flour
1½ teaspoons salt
1½ tablespoons honey
¼ teaspoon baking soda
2 teaspoons Red Star brand
   active dry yeast for all
   machines

1-POUND LOAF

⅓ cup old-fashioned rolled oats
¾ cup buttermilk (or 3
   tablespoons dry buttermilk
   powder and ¾ cup water)
   (for Welbilt machine add 1
   tablespoon more buttermilk)
1 egg
1 cup whole wheat flour
1 cup bread flour
1 teaspoon salt
1 tablespoon honey
¼ teaspoon baking soda
2 teaspoons Red Star brand
   active dry yeast for all
   machines

Place all ingredients in bread pan, select Light Crust setting, and press Start.

After the baking cycle ends, remove bread from pan, place on cake rack, and allow to cool 1 hour before slicing.

```
CRUST: LIGHT
MENU SELECTION: BAKE (LIGHT)
```

·· SWEET OATMEAL BREAD ··

What a nicely shaped loaf this is! To enjoy this lush bread at its best, cut a thick slice and toast it.

1½-POUND LOAF

¾ cup old-fashioned rolled oats
1¼ cups water (for Welbilt/Dak machines add 2 tablespoons more water)
3 cups bread flour
1½ teaspoons salt
3 tablespoons molasses
1½ tablespoons sugar
1½ teaspoons Red Star brand active dry yeast for all machines except 1½-pound Welbilt/Dak machines (use 2 teaspoons yeast)

1-POUND LOAF

½ cup old-fashioned rolled oats
¾ cup water (for Welbilt machine add 1 tablespoon more water)
2 cups bread flour
1 teaspoon salt
2 tablespoons molasses
1 tablespoon sugar
1½ teaspoons Red Star brand active dry yeast for all machines

Place all ingredients in bread pan, select Light Crust setting, and press Start.

After the baking cycle ends, remove bread from pan, place on cake rack, and allow to cool 1 hour before slicing.

CRUST: LIGHT
MENU SELECTION: BAKE (LIGHT)

◆◆ DENNIS'S BLARNEY-STONE ◆◆
BREAD

A husband pleaser, and a loaf to make any Irishman proud, this oat bread gives off a lovely aroma just cutting into it. It has a creamy white interior and a chewy texture.

1½-POUND LOAF

1 cup old-fashioned rolled oats
1¼ cups milk (for Welbilt/Dak machines add 2 tablespoons more milk)
1 egg
3 cups bread flour
1½ teaspoons salt
1½ tablespoons butter or margarine
3 tablespoons honey
1½ teaspoons Red Star brand active dry yeast for all machines except 1½-pound Welbilt/Dak machines (use 2 teaspoons yeast)

1-POUND LOAF

½ cup old-fashioned rolled oats
⅝ cup milk (for Welbilt machine add 1 tablespoon more milk)
1 egg
2 cups bread flour
1 teaspoon salt
1 tablespoon butter or margarine
2 tablespoons honey
1½ teaspoons Red Star brand active dry yeast for all machines

Place all ingredients in bread pan, select Light Crust setting, and press Start.

After the baking cycle ends, remove bread from pan, place on cake rack, and allow to cool 1 hour before slicing.

CRUST: LIGHT
MENU SELECTION: BAKE (LIGHT)

** OLDE ENGLISH BARLEY ** BREAD

The barley flour in this bread imparts a mild, sweet, nutty flavor. It's good toasted or used for sandwiches.

1½-POUND LOAF

½ cup water (for Welbilt/Dak
   machines add 2 tablespoons
   more water)
½ cup milk
1 egg
3 cups bread flour
½ cup barley flour
1½ teaspoons salt
1½ tablespoons oil
1½ tablespoons honey
2 teaspoons Red Star brand
   active dry yeast for all
   machines

1-POUND LOAF

⅜ cup water (for Welbilt
   machine add 1 tablespoon
   more water)
¼ cup milk
1 egg
2 cups bread flour
⅓ cup barley flour
1 teaspoon salt
1 tablespoon oil
1 tablespoon honey
2 teaspoons Red Star brand
   active dry yeast for all
   machines

Place all ingredients in bread pan and press Start.

After the baking cycle ends, remove bread from pan, place on cake rack, and allow to cool 1 hour before slicing.

```
CRUST: REGULAR
MENU SELECTION: BAKE
```

◆◆ WHEAT AND BARLEY BREAD ◆◆

Here's a bread that will appeal to health-minded bread lovers. It has a full-bodied flavor that harmonizes well with any sandwich filling.

1½-POUND LOAF
1⅛ cups water (for Welbilt/Dak
  machines add 2 tablespoons
  more water)
1½ cups bread flour
1½ cups whole wheat flour
½ cup barley flour
1½ teaspoons salt
1½ tablespoons butter or
  margarine
1½ tablespoons molasses
1½ tablespoons nonfat dry milk
  powder
2 teaspoons Red Star brand
  active dry yeast for all
  machines

1-POUND LOAF
⅞ cup water (for Welbilt
  machine add 1 tablespoon
  more water)
1 cup bread flour
1 cup whole wheat flour
⅓ cup barley flour
1 teaspoon salt
1 tablespoon butter or
  margarine
1 tablespoon molasses
1 tablespoon nonfat dry milk
  powder
2 teaspoons Red Star brand
  active dry yeast for all
  machines

Place all ingredients in bread pan and press Start.

After the baking cycle ends, remove bread from pan, place on cake rack, and allow to cool 1 hour before slicing.

```
CRUST: REGULAR
MENU SELECTION: BAKE
```

•• BUCKWHEAT BREAD ••

This bread should satisfy any buckwheat lover in the household. It has a mild buckwheat flavor, making it a good choice for breakfast toast.

1½-POUND LOAF

¼ cup instant potato flakes
⅝ cup milk
⅝ cup water (for Welbilt/Dak machines add 2 tablespoons more water)
2 cups bread flour
1 cup whole wheat flour
⅓ cup buckwheat flour
1½ teaspoons salt
1½ tablespoons butter or margarine
2 tablespoons dark corn syrup
2 teaspoons Red Star brand active dry yeast for all machines

1-POUND LOAF

3 tablespoons instant potato flakes
½ cup milk
⅜ cup water (for Welbilt machine add 1 tablespoon more water)
1½ cups bread flour
½ cup whole wheat flour
¼ cup buckwheat flour
1 teaspoon salt
1 tablespoon butter or margarine
1 tablespoon dark corn syrup
2 teaspoons Red Star brand active dry yeast for all machines

Place all ingredients in bread pan, select Light Crust setting, and press Start.

After the baking cycle ends, remove bread from pan, place on cake rack, and allow to cool 1 hour before slicing.

CRUST: LIGHT
MENU SELECTION: BAKE (LIGHT)

✦✦ SHAYNA'S MILLET BREAD ✦✦

Linda's daughter requests this bread whenever she comes home from college. She's a vegetarian and this bread satisfies her need for nutrition and a hearty taste.

1½-POUND LOAF

*1⅛ cups buttermilk (or 4
   tablespoons dry buttermilk
   powder and 1⅛ cups water)*
*⅜ cup water (for Welbilt/Dak
   machines add 2 tablespoons
   more water)*
2 cups whole wheat flour
1 cup bread flour
¾ cup millet flour
1 teaspoon salt
1½ tablespoons oil
1½ tablespoons honey
¼ teaspoon baking soda
*2 teaspoons Red Star brand
   active dry yeast for all
   machines*

1-POUND LOAF

*¾ cup buttermilk (or 3
   tablespoons dry buttermilk
   powder and ¾ cup water)*
*¼ cup + 1 tablespoon water
   (for Welbilt machine add 1
   tablespoon more water)*
1⅓ cups whole wheat flour
⅔ cup bread flour
½ cup millet flour
1 teaspoon salt
1 tablespoon oil
1 tablespoon honey
¼ teaspoon baking soda
*2 teaspoons Red Star brand
   active dry yeast for all
   machines*

Place all ingredients in bread pan and press Start.

After the baking cycle ends, remove bread from pan, place on cake rack, and allow to cool 1 hour before slicing.

```
CRUST: REGULAR
MENU SELECTION: BAKE
```

·· CHERI'S ORANGE ·· MILLET BREAD

Cheri was our chief bread baker and friend in need during the writing of *Bread Machine Magic*. She baked and tested most of the breads in this book. Of them all, this bread was her favorite. It's a wholesome loaf bursting with different flavors and textures.

1½-POUND LOAF	1-POUND LOAF
⅝ cup water (for Welbilt/Dak machines add 2 tablespoons more water)	⅜ cup water (for Welbilt machine add 1 tablespoon more water)
½ cup orange juice	⅜ cup orange juice
2 cups bread flour	1 cup bread flour
1 cup whole wheat flour	1 cup whole wheat flour
3 tablespoons whole millet	2 tablespoons whole millet
1½ teaspoons salt	1 teaspoon salt
1½ tablespoons butter or margarine	1 tablespoon butter or margarine
1½ tablespoons honey	1 tablespoon honey
3 tablespoons raw, unsalted sunflower seeds	2 tablespoons raw, unsalted sunflower seeds
3 tablespoons raisins	2 tablespoons raisins
Grated rind of 1 orange	Grated rind of ½ orange
3 teaspoons Red Star brand active dry yeast for all machines	1½ teaspoons Red Star brand active dry yeast for all machines

Place all ingredients in bread pan, select Light Crust setting, and press Start.

After the baking cycle ends, remove bread from pan, place on cake rack, and allow to cool 1 hour before slicing.

```
CRUST: LIGHT
MENU SELECTION: BAKE (LIGHT)
```

** SUNNY CALIFORNIA BREAD **

You can almost taste the sunshine in this delightful whole wheat bread. This tall loaf is great for snacking or toasted for breakfast.

1½-POUND LOAF

½ cup orange juice (for Welbilt/
  Dak machines add 2
  tablespoons more juice)
⅜ cup milk
1 egg
2 cups bread flour
1 cup whole wheat flour
1 teaspoon salt
2 tablespoons butter or
  margarine
3 tablespoons sugar
Grated rind of 1 orange
½ cup raw, unsalted sunflower
  seeds
2 teaspoons Red Star brand
  active dry yeast for all
  machines

1-POUND LOAF

⅜ cup orange juice (for Welbilt
  machine add 1 tablespoon
  more juice)
¼ cup milk
1 egg
1⅓ cups bread flour
⅔ cup whole wheat flour
1 teaspoon salt
1½ tablespoons butter or
  margarine
2 tablespoons sugar
Grated rind of ½ orange
⅓ cup raw, unsalted sunflower
  seeds
2 teaspoons Red Star brand
  active dry yeast for all
  machines

Place all ingredients in bread pan, select Light Crust setting, and press Start.

After the baking cycle ends, remove bread from pan, place on cake rack, and allow to cool 1 hour before slicing.

```
CRUST: LIGHT
MENU SELECTION: BAKE (LIGHT)
```

·· SUNFLOWER BREAD ··

Here's another whole-grain bread with a distinctive nutty flavor and texture. It's delicious on the dinner table as well as in the lunchbox.

1½-POUND LOAF	1-POUND LOAF
½ cup old-fashioned rolled oats	⅓ cup old-fashioned rolled oats
½ cup buttermilk (or 2 tablespoons dry buttermilk powder and ½ cup water)	⅜ cup buttermilk (or 2 tablespoons dry buttermilk powder and ⅜ cup water)
½ cup water (for Welbilt/Dak machines add 2 tablespoons more water)	¼ cup water (for Welbilt machine add 1 tablespoon more water)
1 egg	1 egg
2½ cups bread flour	1⅔ cups bread flour
½ cup whole wheat flour	⅓ cup whole wheat flour
1½ teaspoons salt	1 teaspoon salt
1½ tablespoons butter or margarine	1 tablespoon butter or margarine
2 tablespoons honey	1 tablespoon honey
1 tablespoon molasses	2 teaspoons molasses
⅓ cup raw, unsalted sunflower seeds	¼ cup raw, unsalted sunflower seeds
¼ teaspoon baking soda	¼ teaspoon baking soda
2 teaspoons Red Star brand active dry yeast for all machines	1½ teaspoons Red Star brand active dry yeast for all machines

Place all ingredients in bread pan, select Light Crust setting, and press Start.

After the baking cycle ends, remove bread from pan, place on cake rack, and allow to cool 1 hour before slicing.

```
CRUST: LIGHT
MENU SELECTION: BAKE (LIGHT)
```

VEGETABLE
BREADS

•• CARROT-HERB BREAD ••

Get your vitamin A with this beautifully shaped loaf that has a mild carrot flavor. You can vary the amounts of herbs in this bread to suit your own taste. We like the dill so we always add a dash more. This is a superb sandwich bread.

1½-POUND LOAF

½ cup water (for Welbilt/Dak
   machines add 2 tablespoons
   more water)
⅜ cup milk
2 cups whole wheat flour
1 cup bread flour
1½ teaspoons salt
2 tablespoons butter or
   margarine
1½ tablespoons honey
⅔ cup finely grated carrot
¾ teaspoon dried dill
¾ teaspoon dried thyme
¾ teaspoon dried parsley
1½ teaspoons Red Star brand
   active dry yeast for all
   machines except 1½-pound
   Welbilt/Dak machines (use 2
   teaspoons yeast)

1-POUND LOAF

⅓ cup water (for Welbilt
   machine add 1 tablespoon
   more water)
⅓ cup milk
1⅓ cups whole wheat flour
⅔ cup bread flour
1 teaspoon salt
1½ tablespoons butter or
   margarine
1 tablespoon honey
½ cup finely grated carrot
½ teaspoon dried dill
½ teaspoon dried thyme
½ teaspoon dried parsley
1½ teaspoons Red Star brand
   active dry yeast for all
   machines

Place all ingredients in bread pan, select Light Crust setting, and press Start.

After the baking cycle ends, remove bread from pan, place on cake rack, and allow to cool 1 hour before slicing.

```
CRUST: LIGHT
MENU SELECTION: BAKE (LIGHT)
```

•• CRUNCHY CARROT BREAD ••

The kids will love this flavorful, crunchy whole wheat bread. Sliced, it's a great-looking loaf flecked with grated carrot and poppy seeds.

1½-POUND LOAF	1-POUND LOAF
⅞ cup water (for Welbilt/Dak machines add 2 tablespoons more water)	½ cup water (for Welbilt machine add 1 tablespoon more water)
2 cups whole wheat flour	1½ cups whole wheat flour
1 cup bread flour	½ cup bread flour
1½ teaspoons salt	1 teaspoon salt
2 tablespoons butter or margarine	1½ tablespoons butter or margarine
2 tablespoons honey	1 tablespoon honey
1 cup finely grated carrots	⅔ cup finely grated carrots
1 tablespoon poppy seeds	2 teaspoons poppy seeds
2 teaspoons Red Star brand active dry yeast for all machines	2 teaspoons Red Star brand active dry yeast for all machines

Place all ingredients in bread pan, select Light Crust setting, and press Start.

After the baking cycle ends, remove bread from pan, place on cake rack, and allow to cool 1 hour before slicing.

```
CRUST: LIGHT
MENU SELECTION: BAKE (LIGHT)
```

⋆⋆ BROCCOLI-CHEESE BREAD ⋆⋆

This bread will surprise your guests. What fun to have them guess what's in it! It not only tastes exotic but also has a tantalizing aroma as it bakes.

1½-POUND LOAF

1 (10-ounce) package frozen broccoli with cheese sauce

⅜ cup milk (for Welbilt/Dak machines add 2 tablespoons more milk)

1 egg

3 cups bread flour

1 teaspoon salt

1½ tablespoons butter or margarine

¼ cup minced onion

1½ teaspoons Red Star brand active dry yeast for all machines except 1½-pound Welbilt/Dak machines (use 2 teaspoons yeast)

1-POUND LOAF

1 (10-ounce) package frozen broccoli with cheese sauce (for Welbilt machine add 1 tablespoon milk)

1 egg

2 cups bread flour

1 teaspoon salt

1 tablespoon butter or margarine

3 tablespoons minced onion

1½ teaspoons Red Star brand active dry yeast for all machines

Cook the broccoli as directed on the package. Place cooked broccoli in food processor and chop briefly to cut up the large pieces. Allow mixture to cool to room temperature.

Place all ingredients including the broccoli mixture in bread pan and press Start.

After the baking cycle ends, remove bread from pan, place on cake rack, and allow to cool 1 hour before slicing.

```
CRUST: REGULAR
MENU SELECTION: BAKE
```

·· TOMATO BREAD ··

There's no mistaking this one! It's a bright pumpkin color with a very definite tomato flavor. The aroma as it bakes is extraordinary! Leftovers make wonderful croutons.

1½-POUND LOAF

⅝ cup milk (for Welbilt/Dak machines add 2 tablespoons more milk)
1 (6-ounce) can tomato paste
1 egg
3¼ cups bread flour
½ teaspoon salt
1 tablespoon olive oil
1 tablespoon sugar
1 teaspoon Italian seasoning
2 teaspoons dried minced onion
¼ teaspoon garlic powder
½ teaspoon grated nutmeg
1½ teaspoons Red Star brand active dry yeast for all machines except 1½-pound Welbilt/Dak machines (use 2 teaspoons yeast)

1-POUND LOAF

¼ cup milk (for Welbilt machine add 1 tablespoon more milk)
6 tablespoons tomato paste
1 egg
2 cups bread flour
½ teaspoon salt
2 teaspoons olive oil
2 teaspoons sugar
½ teaspoon Italian seasoning
1½ teaspoons dried minced onion
¼ teaspoon garlic powder
¼ teaspoon grated nutmeg
1½ teaspoons Red Star brand active dry yeast for all machines

Place all ingredients in bread pan, select Light Crust setting, and press Start.

After the baking cycle ends, remove bread from pan, place on cake rack, and allow to cool 1 hour before slicing.

```
CRUST: LIGHT
MENU SELECTION: BAKE (LIGHT)
```

·· ELLIOT AND SARA'S RED ·· PEPPER BREAD

This is probably the best of the vegetable breads. For gourmet cooks like Lois's son Elliot and his wife, this bread is good enough to serve to friends as an appetizer. Turn any leftovers into croutons for a special soup or salad.

1½-POUND LOAF	1-POUND LOAF
½ cup water (for Welbilt/Dak machines add 2 tablespoons more water)	½ cup water (for Welbilt machine add 1 tablespoon more water)
¼ cup tomato juice	3 tablespoons tomato juice
2½ cups bread flour	1⅔ cups bread flour
½ cup whole wheat flour	⅓ cup whole wheat flour
1½ teaspoons salt	1 teaspoon salt
1½ tablespoons butter or margarine	1 tablespoon butter or margarine
2 tablespoons molasses	1 tablespoon molasses
½ cup minced red bell pepper	⅓ cup minced red bell pepper
1½ teaspoons dried tarragon	1 teaspoon dried tarragon
1½ teaspoons Red Star brand active dry yeast for all machines except 1½-pound Welbilt/Dak machines (use 2 teaspoons yeast)	1½ teaspoons Red Star brand active dry yeast for all machines

Place all ingredients in bread pan, select Light Crust setting, and press Start.

After the baking cycle ends, remove bread from pan, place on cake rack, and allow to cool 1 hour before slicing.

CRUST: LIGHT
MENU SELECTION: BAKE (LIGHT)

·· ONION SOUP BREAD ··

This bread smells so terrific while baking that it's hard waiting long enough to let it cool before slicing into it! A glorious onion flavor makes this an excellent addition to your next barbecue meal.

1½-POUND LOAF

¼ cup milk
¼ cup water (for Welbilt/Dak
   machines add 2 tablespoons
   more water)
1 egg
½ cup sour cream
3 cups bread flour
1 tablespoon butter or
   margarine
1 tablespoon sugar
2½ tablespoons dry onion soup
   mix
1½ teaspoons Red Star brand
   active dry yeast for all
   machines except 1½-pound
   Welbilt/Dak machines (use 2
   teaspoons yeast)

1-POUND LOAF

⅛ cup milk
⅛ cup water (for Welbilt
   machine add 1 tablespoon
   more water)
1 egg
⅓ cup sour cream
2 cups bread flour
2 teaspoons butter or margarine
2 teaspoons sugar
2 tablespoons dry onion soup
   mix
1½ teaspoons Red Star brand
   active dry yeast for all
   machines

Place all ingredients in bread pan, select Light Crust setting, and press Start.

After the baking cycle ends, remove bread from pan, place on cake rack, and allow to cool 1 hour before slicing.

```
CRUST: LIGHT
MENU SELECTION: BAKE (LIGHT)
```

ᐧᐧ JALAPEÑO CHEESE BREAD ᐧᐧ

Wow—hot stuff! Serve this coarsely textured, very spicy bread at your next cocktail party and watch it disappear. It's great with a glass of wine or a cold beer, but its perfect partner is a frosty margarita!

1½-POUND LOAF

¾ cup sour cream
⅛ cup water (for Welbilt/Dak
  machines add 2 tablespoons
  more water)
1 egg
3 cups all-purpose flour
1½ teaspoons salt
2 tablespoons sugar
¼ teaspoon baking soda
1 cup (4 ounces) grated sharp
  Cheddar cheese
3 tablespoons seeded and
  chopped fresh jalapeño
  pepper (about 4 peppers) or
  canned diced jalapeño
  peppers
1½ teaspoons Red Star brand
  active dry yeast for all
  machines except 1½-pound
  Welbilt/Dak machines (use 2
  teaspoons yeast)

1-POUND LOAF

½ cup sour cream
⅛ cup water (for Welbilt
  machine add 1 tablespoon
  more water)
1 egg
2 cups all-purpose flour
1 teaspoon salt
1½ tablespoons sugar
¼ teaspoon baking soda
¾ cup (3 ounces) grated sharp
  Cheddar cheese
2 tablespoons seeded and
  chopped fresh jalapeño
  pepper (about 3 peppers) or
  canned diced jalapeño
  peppers
1½ teaspoons Red Star brand
  active dry yeast for all
  machines

Place all ingredients in bread pan, select Light Crust setting, and press Start.

After the baking cycle ends, remove bread from pan, place on cake rack, and allow to cool 1 hour before slicing.

CRUST: LIGHT
MENU SELECTION: BAKE (LIGHT)

** AUTUMN HARVEST BREAD **

Welcome in the fall season with this delightful bread that's a perfect combination of autumn's colorful fruits and vegetables. This tender, slightly tangy bread is delectable served with an orange butter.

1½-POUND LOAF	1-POUND LOAF
½ cup diced carrots, cooked, pureed	⅓ cup diced carrots, cooked, pureed
½ cup canned pumpkin or diced banana squash, cooked, pureed	⅓ cup canned pumpkin or diced banana squash, cooked, pureed
½ cup unsweetened applesauce	⅓ cup unsweetened applesauce
¼ cup carrot water* (for Welbilt/ Dak machines add 2 tablespoons more water)	(for Welbilt machine add 1 tablespoon water)
1½ cups whole wheat flour	1 cup whole wheat flour
1½ cups bread flour	1 cup bread flour
1½ teaspoons salt	1 teaspoon salt
1½ tablespoons butter or margarine	1 tablespoon butter or margarine
2 tablespoons honey	1 tablespoon honey
¼ teaspoon ground allspice	¼ teaspoon ground allspice
2 teaspoons Red Star brand active dry yeast for all machines	2 teaspoons Red Star brand active dry yeast for all machines

Place all ingredients in bread pan, select Light Crust setting, and press Start.

After the baking cycle ends, remove bread from pan, place on cake rack, and allow to cool 1 hour before slicing.

```
CRUST: LIGHT
MENU SELECTION: BAKE (LIGHT)
```

*The water in which you cooked the carrots.

·· I YAM WHAT I YAM BREAD ··

Friends will ask, "What's in this bread?" It has a lovely golden color and a sweet, elusive taste. It would be an elegant addition to your Thanksgiving dinner, but don't wait until then to try it.

1½-POUND LOAF

½ cup milk (for Welbilt/Dak machines add 2 tablespoons more milk)

1 egg

½ cup drained and chopped canned yams

3 cups bread flour

1½ teaspoons salt

1½ tablespoons butter or margarine

2 tablespoons brown sugar

⅓ cup mini marshmallows (optional)

1½ teaspoons Red Star brand active dry yeast for all machines except 1½-pound Welbilt/Dak machines (use 2 teaspoons yeast)

1-POUND LOAF

⅜ cup milk (for Welbilt machine add 1 tablespoon more milk)

1 egg

¼ cup drained and chopped canned yams

2 cups bread flour

1 teaspoon salt

1 tablespoon butter or margarine

1 tablespoon brown sugar

¼ cup mini marshmallows (optional)

1½ teaspoons Red Star brand active dry yeast for all machines

Place all ingredients in bread pan and press Start.

After the baking cycle ends, remove bread from pan, place on cake rack, and allow to cool 1 hour before slicing.

```
CRUST: REGULAR
MENU SELECTION: BAKE
```

•• ZUCCHINI-CARROT BREAD ••

The carrot, zucchini, and spices in this deceptive loaf of bread make it seem highly sweetened; it isn't. You can eat that second slice without guilt.

1½-POUND LOAF

¾ cup water (for Welbilt/Dak machines add 2 tablespoons more water)

3 cups bread flour

1½ teaspoons salt

1½ tablespoons butter or margarine

1½ tablespoons honey

1½ tablespoons nonfat dry milk powder

⅓ cup grated zucchini

⅓ cup grated carrot

1½ teaspoons ground cinnamon

¾ teaspoon ground cloves

1½ teaspoons Red Star brand active dry yeast for all machines except 1½-pound Welbilt/Dak machines (use 2 teaspoons yeast)

1-POUND LOAF

½ cup water (for Welbilt machine add 1 tablespoon more water)

2 cups bread flour

1 teaspoon salt

1 tablespoon butter or margarine

1 tablespoon honey

1 tablespoon nonfat dry milk powder

¼ cup grated zucchini

¼ cup grated carrot

1 teaspoon ground cinnamon

½ teaspoon ground cloves

1½ teaspoons Red Star brand active dry yeast for all machines

Place all ingredients in bread pan, select Light Crust setting, and press Start.

After the baking cycle ends, remove bread from pan, place on cake rack, and allow to cool 1 hour before slicing.

```
CRUST: LIGHT
MENU SELECTION: BAKE (LIGHT)
```

•• ZUCCHINI WHEAT BREAD ••

The zucchini adds moisture and a comforting flavor to this nutritious bread.

1½-POUND LOAF

¼ cup milk (for Welbilt/Dak
machines add 2 tablespoons
more milk)
1 egg
2¼ cups bread flour
¾ cup whole wheat flour
¼ cup wheat germ
1½ teaspoons salt
1½ tablespoons butter or
margarine
1½ tablespoons brown sugar
1½ cups shredded zucchini
2 teaspoons ground coriander
1½ teaspoons Red Star brand
active dry yeast for all
machines except 1½-pound
Welbilt/Dak machines (use 2
teaspoons yeast)

1-POUND LOAF

3 tablespoons milk (for Welbilt
machine add 1 tablespoon
more milk)
1 egg
1½ cup bread flour
½ cup whole wheat flour
3 tablespoons wheat germ
1 teaspoon salt
1 tablespoon butter or
margarine
1 tablespoon brown sugar
1 cup shredded zucchini
1 teaspoon ground coriander
1½ teaspoons Red Star brand
active dry yeast for all
machines

Place all ingredients in bread pan, select Light Crust setting, and press Start.

After the baking cycle ends, remove bread from pan, place on cake rack, and allow to cool 1 hour before slicing.

CRUST: LIGHT
MENU SELECTION: BAKE (LIGHT)

FRUIT BREADS

•• ALOHA BREAD ••

This is a delightful whole wheat bread with a surprising flavor of the tropics. It is wonderful in a bread pudding or as french toast.

1½-POUND LOAF

¾ cup buttermilk (for Welbilt/ Dak machines no extra water is needed)
2 cups whole wheat flour
1 cup bread flour
1 teaspoon salt
1½ tablespoons butter or margarine
3 tablespoons sugar
¼ teaspoon baking soda
1 (8-ounce) can crushed pineapple, well drained
⅓ cup flaked coconut
1½ teaspoons Red Star brand active dry yeast for all machines except 1½-pound Welbilt/Dak machines (use 2 teaspoons yeast)

1-POUND LOAF

½ cup buttermilk (for Welbilt machine no extra water is needed)
1⅓ cups whole wheat flour
⅔ cup bread flour
½ teaspoon salt
1 tablespoon butter or margarine
2 tablespoons sugar
¼ teaspoon baking soda
1 (8-ounce) can crushed pineapple, well drained
¼ cup flaked coconut
1½ teaspoons Red Star brand active dry yeast for all machines

Place all ingredients in bread pan, select Light Crust setting, and press Start.

After the baking cycle ends, remove bread from pan, place on cake rack, and allow to cool 1 hour before slicing.

```
CRUST: LIGHT
MENU SELECTION: BAKE (LIGHT)
```

◆◆ SUNDAY MORNING ◆◆
APRICOT BREAD

This is a welcome addition to the breakfast table but don't wait for Sunday morning; it's great every day. This bread is well received as a gift. Everyone seems to like the strong apricot flavor.

1½-POUND LOAF

½ cup old-fashioned rolled oats
1 cup buttermilk (or 4 tablespoons dry buttermilk powder and 1 cup water) (for Welbilt/Dak machines add 2 tablespoons more buttermilk)
1 egg
2 cups bread flour
1 cup whole wheat flour
1 teaspoon salt
2 tablespoons butter or margarine
¼ cup apricot preserves
½ cup chopped dried apricots
1½ teaspoons Red Star brand active dry yeast for all machines except 1½-pound Welbilt/Dak machines (use 2 teaspoons yeast)

1-POUND LOAF

⅓ cup old-fashioned rolled oats
⅝ cup buttermilk (or 3 tablespoons dry buttermilk powder and ⅝ cup water) (for Welbilt machine add 1 tablespoon more buttermilk)
1 egg
1⅓ cups bread flour
⅔ cup whole wheat flour
1 teaspoon salt
1½ tablespoons butter or margarine
3 tablespoons apricot preserves
⅓ cup chopped dried apricots
1½ teaspoons Red Star brand active dry yeast for all machines

Place all ingredients in bread pan, select Light Crust setting, and press Start.

After the baking cycle ends, remove bread from pan, place on cake rack, and allow to cool 1 hour before slicing.

```
CRUST: LIGHT
MENU SELECTION: BAKE (LIGHT)
```

•• CRUNCHY MUNCHY BREAD ••

The peanut butter flavor in this bread is so yummy, there's no need to adorn it. It's perfect as an after-school snack. Hint: If your apples are very moist or if the weather is quite humid, you might want to add 2 to 4 extra teaspoons of bread flour as the dough mixes.

1½-POUND LOAF

1⅛ cups milk (for Welbilt/Dak machines no extra milk is needed)
2 cups whole wheat flour
1 cup bread flour
1 teaspoon salt
¼ cup chunky peanut butter
2 tablespoons honey
1 cup cored and chopped, unpeeled Granny Smith apple
¼ cup chopped unsalted peanuts
2 teaspoons Red Star brand active dry yeast for all machines except 1½-pound Welbilt/Dak machines (use 2 teaspoons yeast)

1-POUND LOAF

⅞ cup milk (for Welbilt machine add 1 tablespoon more milk)
1 cup whole wheat flour
1½ cups bread flour
½ teaspoon salt
3 tablespoons chunky peanut butter
1 tablespoon honey
½ cup cored and chopped, unpeeled Granny Smith apple
2 tablespoons chopped unsalted peanuts
1½ teaspoons Red Star brand active dry yeast for all machines

Place all ingredients in bread pan, select Light Crust setting, and press Start.

After the baking cycle ends, remove bread from pan, place on cake rack, and allow to cool 1 hour before slicing.

```
CRUST: LIGHT
MENU SELECTION: BAKE (LIGHT)
```

•• JOHNNY APPLESEED BREAD ••

This is a sweet, chewy bread with a strong, delicious taste of apples. Try it toasted some morning. For best results in the one-pound Welbilt machine, use ½ cup of apple juice.

1½-POUND LOAF

½ cup apple juice (for Welbilt/
  Dak machines add 3
  tablespoons more juice)
½ cup unsweetened applesauce
3 cups bread flour
1½ teaspoons salt
1½ tablespoons butter or
  margarine
3 tablespoons brown sugar
½ cup cored, peeled, and
  chopped Granny Smith apple
¼ cup raisins (optional)
½ teaspoon ground cinnamon
Pinch of grated nutmeg
1½ teaspoons Red Star brand
  active dry yeast for all
  machines except 1½-pound
  Welbilt/Dak machines (use 2
  teaspoons yeast)

1-POUND LOAF

⅓ cup apple juice
⅓ cup unsweetened applesauce
2 cups bread flour
1 teaspoon salt
1 tablespoon butter or
  margarine
2 tablespoons brown sugar
⅓ cup cored, peeled, and
  chopped Granny Smith apple
3 tablespoons raisins (optional)
½ teaspoon ground cinnamon
Pinch of grated nutmeg
1½ teaspoons Red Star brand
  active dry yeast for all
  machines

Place all ingredients in bread pan, select Light Crust setting, and press Start.

After the baking cycle ends, remove bread from pan, place on cake rack, and allow to cool 1 hour before slicing.

```
CRUST: LIGHT
MENU SELECTION: BAKE (LIGHT)
```

▪▪ BANANA OATMEAL BREAD ▪▪

You'll be proud of this bread because it's beautifully shaped and luscious tasting. Each slice is moist and bursting with banana flavor.

1½-POUND LOAF

1 cup old-fashioned rolled oats

1 egg

¼ cup sour cream (for Welbilt/ Dak machines add 2 tablespoons water)

2 cups sliced ripe banana (about 3 medium)

2 cups bread flour

1 cup whole wheat flour

1 teaspoon salt

1 tablespoon butter or margarine

2 tablespoons honey

1 tablespoon nonfat dry milk powder

½ teaspoon ground cinnamon

¼ teaspoon grated nutmeg

2 teaspoons Red Star brand active dry yeast for all machines

1-POUND LOAF

½ cup old-fashioned rolled oats

1 egg

3 tablespoons sour cream (for Welbilt machine add 1 tablespoon water)

1 cup sliced ripe banana (about 1 large)

1⅓ cups bread flour

⅔ cup whole wheat flour

½ teaspoon salt

2 teaspoons butter or margarine

1½ tablespoons honey

2 teaspoons nonfat dry milk powder

½ teaspoon ground cinnamon

¼ teaspoon grated nutmeg

2 teaspoons Red Star brand active dry yeast for all machines

Place all ingredients in bread pan, select Light Crust setting, and press Start.

After the baking cycle ends, remove bread from pan, place on cake rack, and allow to cool 1 hour before slicing.

```
CRUST: LIGHT
MENU SELECTION: BAKE (LIGHT)
```

•• ANNE AND BILL'S APPLE ••
OATMEAL BREAD
WITH RAISINS

Oatmeal and applesauce combine to make this a lush, rich-tasting loaf. It's a good snack for children and great for breakfast toast.

1½-POUND LOAF

½ cups old-fashioned rolled oats
⅝ cup water (for Welbilt/Dak
  machines add 1 tablespoon
  more water)
½ cup unsweetened applesauce
2¾ cups bread flour
1½ teaspoons salt
1½ tablespoons butter or
  margarine
2 tablespoons brown sugar
1½ tablespoons nonfat dry milk
  powder
⅓ cup raisins
1 teaspoon ground cinnamon
1½ teaspoons Red Star brand
  active dry yeast for all
  machines except 1½-pound
  Welbilt/Dak machines (use 2
  teaspoons yeast)

1-POUND LOAF

⅓ cup old-fashioned rolled oats
½ cup water (for Welbilt
  machine add 1 tablespoon
  more water)
⅓ cup unsweetened applesauce
1¾ cup bread flour
1 teaspoon salt
1 tablespoon butter or
  margarine
1 tablespoon brown sugar
1 tablespoon nonfat dry milk
  powder
¼ cup raisins
1 teaspoon ground cinnamon
1½ teaspoons Red Star brand
  active dry yeast for all
  machines

Place all ingredients in bread pan, select Light Crust setting, and press Start.

After the baking cycle ends, remove bread from pan, place on cake rack, and allow to cool 1 hour before slicing.

CRUST: LIGHT
MENU SELECTION: BAKE (LIGHT)

✦✦ GRANOLA DATE BREAD ✦✦

We experimented with several different types of granola from our local health-food store. The plain granola made a very tasty loaf of bread but a raspberry apple granola turned this into an extraordinary breakfast bread!

1½-POUND LOAF	1-POUND LOAF
½ cup granola	⅓ cup granola
¾ cup buttermilk (or 3 tablespoons dry buttermilk powder and ¾ cup water)	½ cup buttermilk (or 2 tablespoons dry buttermilk powder and ½ cup water)
½ cup water (for Welbilt/Dak machines add 2 tablespoons more water)	⅜ cup water (for Welbilt machine add 1 tablespoon more water)
2 cups bread flour	1 cup bread flour
1 cup whole wheat flour	1 cup whole wheat flour
1½ teaspoons salt	1 teaspoon salt
1½ tablespoons butter or margarine	1 tablespoon butter or margarine
2 tablespoons honey	1½ tablespoons honey
⅓ cup chopped dates	¼ cup chopped dates
¼ teaspoon baking soda	¼ teaspoon baking soda
2 teaspoons Red Star brand active dry yeast for all machines	1½ teaspoons Red Star brand active dry yeast for all machines

Place all ingredients in bread pan, select Light Crust setting, and press Start.

After the baking cycle ends, remove bread from pan, place on cake rack, and allow to cool 1 hour before slicing.

```
CRUST: LIGHT
MENU SELECTION: BAKE (LIGHT)
```

•• MIXED FRUIT BREAD ••

If any of your friends doesn't care for the traditional gift of holiday fruitcake, this bread is a nice alternative.

1½-POUND LOAF
½ cup 100% bran cereal
1 cup buttermilk (or 4
   tablespoons dry buttermilk
   powder and 1 cup water) (for
   Welbilt/Dak machines add 2
   tablespoons more buttermilk)
1 egg
3 cups bread flour
1 teaspoon salt
1½ tablespoons butter or
   margarine
2 tablespoons honey
⅔ cup mixed dried fruits, finely
   chopped
¼ teaspoon ground cinnamon
¼ teaspoon baking soda
2 teaspoons Red Star brand
   active dry yeast for all
   machines

1-POUND LOAF
⅓ cup 100% bran cereal
⅝ cup buttermilk (or 3
   tablespoons dry buttermilk
   powder and ⅝ cup water)
   (for Welbilt machine add 1
   tablespoon more buttermilk)
1 egg
2 cups bread flour
½ teaspoon salt
1 tablespoon butter or
   margarine
1 tablespoon honey
½ cup mixed dried fruits, finely
   chopped
¼ teaspoon ground cinnamon
¼ teaspoon baking soda
2 teaspoons Red Star brand
   active dry yeast for all
   machines

Place all ingredients in bread pan, select Light Crust setting, and press Start.

After the baking cycle ends, remove bread from pan, place on cake rack, and allow to cool 1 hour before slicing.

```
CRUST: LIGHT
MENU SELECTION: BAKE (LIGHT)
```

⁕⁕ ORANGE BREAD ⁕⁕

After much trial and error in testing orange breads, we finally came up with a winner. Try it with chicken salad or as a breakfast toast.

1½-POUND LOAF

1 cup peeled, chopped navel orange
¼ cup orange juice (for Welbilt/ Dak machines add 2 tablespoons more juice)
1 egg
3 cups bread flour
1 teaspoon salt
1 tablespoon butter or margarine
¼ cup orange marmalade
Grated rind of 3 oranges
⅓ cup slivered almonds
2 teaspoons Red Star brand active dry yeast for all machines

1-POUND LOAF

¾ cup peeled, chopped navel orange
1 tablespoon orange juice (for Welbilt machine add 1 tablespoon more juice)
1 egg
2 cups bread flour
1 teaspoon salt
1 tablespoon butter or margarine
3 tablespoons orange marmalade
Grated rind of 2 oranges
¼ cup slivered almonds
2 teaspoons Red Star brand active dry yeast for all machines

Place all ingredients in bread pan, select Light Crust setting, and press Start.

After the baking cycle ends, remove bread from pan, place on cake rack, and allow to cool 1 hour before slicing.

```
CRUST: LIGHT
MENU SELECTION: BAKE (LIGHT)
```

◆◆ MARMALADE AND ◆◆
OATS BREAD

Here's another winner. It's a beautiful-looking loaf, and the combination of orange marmalade and oatmeal makes it very tender, moist, and rich-tasting.

1½-POUND LOAF

⅔ cup old-fashioned rolled oats
1⅛ cups milk (for Welbilt/Dak
    machines add 2 tablespoons
    more milk)
3 cups bread flour
1½ teaspoons salt
1½ tablespoons butter or
    margarine
½ cup orange marmalade
1½ teaspoons Red Star brand
    active dry yeast for all
    machines except 1½-pound
    Welbilt/Dak machines (use 2
    teaspoons yeast)

1-POUND LOAF

½ cup old-fashioned rolled oats
⅞ cups milk (for Welbilt
    machine add 1 tablespoon
    more milk)
2 cups bread flour
1 teaspoon salt
1 tablespoon butter or
    margarine
⅓ cup orange marmalade
1½ teaspoons Red Star brand
    active dry yeast for all
    machines

Place all ingredients in bread pan, select Light Crust setting, and press Start.

After the baking cycle ends, remove bread from pan, place on cake rack, and allow to cool 1 hour before slicing.

```
CRUST: LIGHT
MENU SELECTION: BAKE (LIGHT)
```

•• ERIC AND JANEY'S POPPY-SEED ••
PEACH BREAD

During their recent visit, Lois's son and daughter-in-law sampled this fruit bread fresh from the machine, and loved it. But this bread has us baffled. It has a lovely peach flavor the first few days but if kept longer than that in the freezer, the peach flavor disappears. So, eat it right away!

1½-POUND LOAF	1-POUND LOAF
¼ cup buttermilk (for Welbilt/ Dak machines add 2 tablespoons more buttermilk)	3 tablespoons buttermilk (for Welbilt machine add 1 tablespoon more buttermilk)
2¼ cups bread flour	1½ cups bread flour
1 cup whole wheat flour	⅔ cup whole wheat flour
1½ teaspoons salt	1 teaspoon salt
1½ tablespoons butter or margarine	1 tablespoon butter or margarine
3 tablespoons sugar	2 tablespoons sugar
3 tablespoons brown sugar	2 tablespoons brown sugar
1½ cups pitted, peeled, and chopped peaches (fresh, frozen or canned, well drained)	1 cup pitted, peeled, and chopped peaches (fresh, frozen or canned, well drained)
1 tablespoon poppy seeds	2 teaspoons poppy seeds
1½ teaspoons Red Star brand active dry yeast for all machines except 1½-pound Welbilt/Dak machines (use 2 teaspoons yeast)	1½ teaspoons Red Star brand active dry yeast for all machines

Place all ingredients in bread pan, select Light Crust setting, and press Start.

After the baking cycle ends, remove bread from pan, place on cake rack, and allow to cool 1 hour before slicing.

```
CRUST: LIGHT
MENU SELECTION: BAKE (LIGHT)
```

✦✦ PEACHES AND SPICE BREAD ✦✦

What a sensational taste this peach bread has! It's a tall and beautifully shaped gift bread. If you don't give it away, toast it or try it in a bread pudding.

1½-POUND LOAF

1 cup old-fashioned rolled oats
¼ cup apple juice or the reserved juice from canned peaches (for Welbilt/Dak machines add 2 tablespoons more juice)
1 egg
1½ cups whole wheat flour
1½ cups bread flour
¼ cup miller's bran
1½ teaspoons salt
1½ tablespoons butter or margarine
2 tablespoons honey
1½ cups peeled, pitted, and chopped peaches (fresh, frozen, or canned, well drained)
1 teaspoon ground cinnamon
1 teaspoon ground ginger
1 teaspoon grated nutmeg
⅓ cup chopped walnuts
2 teaspoons Red Star brand active dry yeast for all machines

1-POUND LOAF

½ cup old-fashioned rolled oats
2 tablespoons apple juice or the reserved juice from canned peaches (for Welbilt machine add 1 tablespoon more juice)
1 egg
1 cup whole wheat flour
1 cup bread flour
3 tablespoons miller's bran
1 teaspoon salt
1 tablespoon butter or margarine
1 tablespoon honey
1 cup peeled, pitted, and chopped peaches (fresh, frozen, or canned, well drained)
¾ teaspoon ground cinnamon
¾ teaspoon ground ginger
¾ teaspoon grated nutmeg
¼ cup chopped walnuts
2 teaspoons Red Star brand active dry yeast for all machines

Place all ingredients in bread pan, select Light Crust setting, and press Start.

After the baking cycle ends, remove bread from pan, place on cake rack, and allow to cool 1 hour before slicing.

CRUST: LIGHT
MENU SELECTION: BAKE (LIGHT)

•• SWEET LELANI BREAD ••

This Hawaiian-style bread is a spectacular addition to any luncheon buffet. It's moist, light, and elegant. Don't let the long list of ingredients prevent you from trying this bread. It's definitely one of the best in the book.

1½-POUND LOAF

½ cup canned pineapple
   chunks, cut up and well
   drained (reserve juice)
¼ cup buttermilk (or 1
   tablespoon dry buttermilk
   powder and ¼ cup water)
   (for Welbilt/Dak machines add
   2 tablespoons more
   buttermilk)
¼ cup reserved pineapple juice
1 egg
½ cup sliced banana
3 cups bread flour
¼ cup whole wheat flour
1 teaspoon salt
3 tablespoons butter or
   margarine
1½ tablespoons sugar
½ cup shredded coconut
⅓ cup chopped macadamia
   nuts
¼ teaspoon baking soda
1½ teaspoons Red Star brand
   active dry yeast for all
   machines except 1½-pound
   Welbilt/Dak machines (use 2
   teaspoons yeast)

1-POUND LOAF

⅓ cup canned pineapple
   chunks, cut up and well
   drained (reserve juice)
3 tablespoons buttermilk (or 1
   tablespoon dry buttermilk
   powder and 3 tablespoons
   water) (for Welbilt machine
   add 1 tablespoon more
   buttermilk)
2 tablespoons reserved
   pineapple juice
1 egg
⅓ cup sliced banana
2 cups bread flour
3 tablespoons whole wheat flour
1 teaspoon salt
2 tablespoons butter or
   margarine
1 tablespoon sugar
⅓ cup shredded coconut
¼ cup chopped macadamia
   nuts
¼ teaspoon baking soda
1½ teaspoons Red Star brand
   active dry yeast for all
   machines

Place all ingredients in bread pan, select Light Crust setting, and press Start.

After the baking cycle ends, remove bread from pan, place on cake rack, and allow to cool 1 hour before slicing.

```
CRUST: LIGHT
MENU SELECTION: BAKE (LIGHT)
```

DINNER ROLLS

HOW TO SHAPE DINNER ROLLS ◆◆◆◆◆◆◆◆◆◆

PAN ROLLS

Grease a $9 \times 13 \times 2$-inch pan or a 9-inch round or square cake pan. Gently roll and stretch dough into a log shape. With a sharp knife, divide dough into the desired number of rolls. Roll each piece into a ball and place close together in pan. Cover and let rise in a warm oven 30 to 45 minutes until doubled. Bake as directed in recipe.

CLOVERLEAF ROLLS

Grease a 12-cup muffin tin. Gently roll and stretch dough into a log shape. With a sharp knife, divide dough into the desired number of rolls. Cut each roll into thirds. Roll each piece of dough into small balls; place 3 in each greased muffin cup. Cover and let rise in a warm oven 30 to 45 minutes until doubled. Bake as directed in recipe.

For Easy Cloverleaf Rolls, don't cut rolls into thirds. Instead, roll up each piece of dough into a ball and place each in a greased muffin cup. With clean scissors dipped in flour, cut the top of each roll in half, then in quarters. Cover and let rise as above.

SNAILS

Grease a large baking sheet. Stretch dough into a log shape and with a sharp knife, divide dough into the desired number of rolls. Roll each piece into a 12-inch rope. Hold one end of the rope (the center of the snail) in place on the baking sheet. Coil the rest of the rope around the center; tuck the end underneath. Cover and let rise in a warm oven 30 to 45 minutes until doubled. Bake as directed in recipe. (Optional: Before baking, brush rolls with beaten egg; sprinkle with sesame or poppy seeds.)

BUTTERHORNS AND CRESCENT ROLLS

Grease a large baking sheet. With a sharp knife, divide 1½-pound dough into thirds; divide 1-pound dough in half. Roll each piece into an 8- or 9-inch circle. With a knife or pizza cutter, divide each circle into 8 wedges, as if cutting a pizza. Separate the wedges. Starting at the wide end, roll up each wedge toward the point. Place on baking sheet with points underneath. For crescent rolls, curve each roll on the baking sheet into a crescent shape by bringing the points slightly toward each other. Cover and let rise in a warm oven 30 to 45 minutes until doubled. Bake as directed in recipe.

PARKER HOUSE ROLLS

Grease a large baking sheet. With a rolling pin, roll out dough to a ¼ inch thickness. With a 2- to 2½-inch biscuit cutter, cut out rolls. Brush each with melted butter. Holding both ends of a clean pen or pencil, press it into each roll slightly off center to make a crease. Fold the larger side over the smaller side; press the edges together lightly. Place on baking sheet. Cover and let rise in a warm oven 30 to 45 minutes until doubled. Bake as directed in the recipe.

FAN TANS

Butter a 12-cup muffin tin. With a rolling pin, roll dough into a 9 × 12-inch rectangle. Brush with melted butter. With a sharp knife, cut 6 lengthwise strips about 1½ inches wide. Stack strips on top of each other, then cut crosswise into twelve 1-inch pieces. Place cut side down in buttered muffin cups. Cover and let rise in a warm oven 20 to 30 minutes until almost doubled. Bake as directed in recipe.

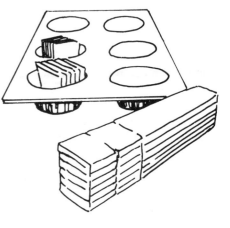

✦✦ DINNER ROLLS ✦✦

These tasty four-star rolls will disappear from the table before they're even cool.

1½-POUND

¾ cup water (for Welbilt/Dak machines add 2 tablespoons more water)

1 egg

3 cups all-purpose flour

1½ teaspoons salt

3 tablespoons butter or margarine

3 tablespoons sugar

3 tablespoons nonfat dry milk powder

1½ teaspoons Red Star brand active dry yeast for all machines except 1½-pound Welbilt/Dak machines (use 2 teaspoons yeast)

2 tablespoons melted butter or margarine

1-POUND

½ cup water (for Welbilt machine add 1 tablespoon more water)

1 egg

2 cups all-purpose flour

1 teaspoon salt

2 tablespoons butter or margarine

2 tablespoons sugar

2 tablespoons nonfat dry milk powder

1½ teaspoons Red Star brand active dry yeast for all machines

2 tablespoons melted butter or margarine

Place all ingredients except melted butter in bread pan, select Dough setting, and press Start.

Grease a large baking sheet.

When dough has risen long enough, the machine will beep. Turn off bread machine, remove bread pan, and turn out dough onto a floured countertop or cutting board. Gently roll and stretch dough into an 18-inch rope.

FOR 1½-POUND

With a sharp knife, divide dough into 12 to 18 pieces.

FOR 1-POUND

With a sharp knife, divide dough into 8 to 12 pieces.

Form dough into desired roll shapes (see pages 105–106). Place rolls on baking sheet; cover and let rise in warm oven 30 to 45 minutes until doubled. (Hint: To warm oven slightly, turn oven on Warm setting for 2 minutes, then turn it off, and place covered rolls in oven to rise. Remove sheet from oven to preheat.)

Preheat oven to 400°F. Brush rolls with melted butter; bake for 12 to 15 minutes until brown. Remove from oven; serve warm.

1½-pound dough yields 12 to 18 rolls
1-pound dough yields 8 to 12 rolls

MENU SELECTION: DOUGH

◆◆ POTATO ROLLS ◆◆

These homestyle rolls are crusty on the outside, tender and flavorful inside.

1½-POUND

¾ cup water (for Welbilt/Dak
    machines add 2 tablespoons
    more water)
1 egg
3 cups all-purpose flour
½ cup plain mashed potatoes,
    cooled
1 teaspoon salt
¼ cup shortening
¼ cup sugar
1½ teaspoons Red Star brand
    active dry yeast for all
    machines except 1½-pound
    Welbilt/Dak machines (use 2
    teaspoons yeast)

1-POUND

½ cup water (for Welbilt
    machine add 1 tablespoon
    more water)
1 egg
2 cups all-purpose flour
⅓ cup plain mashed potatoes,
    cooled
1 teaspoon salt
3 tablespoons shortening
3 tablespoons sugar
1½ teaspoons Red Star brand
    active dry yeast for all
    machines

Place all ingredients in bread pan, select Dough setting, and press Start.

When dough has risen long enough, the machine will beep. Turn off bread machine, remove bread pan, and turn out dough onto a heavily floured countertop or cutting board.

FOR 1½-POUND

Gently roll and stretch dough into a 24-inch rope. With a sharp knife, divide dough into 72 pieces. (Hint: First cut dough into 12 equal pieces, then cut each of those into 6 tiny pieces.)

FOR 1-POUND

Gently roll and stretch dough into an 18-inch rope. With a sharp knife, divide dough into 54 pieces. (Hint: First cut dough into 9 equal pieces, then cut each of those into 6 tiny pieces.)

Grease two 12-cup muffin tins. Roll each piece into a ball and place 3 balls in each greased muffin cup. Cover and let rise in a warm oven 30 to 45 minutes until doubled. (Hint: To warm oven slightly, turn oven on Warm setting for 2 minutes, then turn it off, and place covered rolls in oven to rise. Remove tin from oven to preheat.)

Preheat oven to 400°F. Bake 12 minutes until golden. Remove from oven and serve warm.

1½-pound dough yields 24 rolls
1-pound dough yields 18 rolls

MENU SELECTION: DOUGH

** HONEY WHEAT ROLLS **

These dinner rolls are far superior to any packaged rolls you can buy. They're lovely on the Thanksgiving table, and also very popular as a snack fresh out of the oven, split in half, and filled with a small piece of thinly sliced ham and a dab of mustard. Either way, they disappear in a hurry!

1½-POUND	1-POUND
¾ cup water (for Welbilt/Dak machines add 2 tablespoons more water)	½ cup water (for Welbilt machine add 1 tablespoon more water)
1 egg	1 egg
2 cups all-purpose flour	1⅓ cups all-purpose flour
1 cup whole wheat flour	⅔ cup whole wheat flour
1 teaspoon salt	½ teaspoon salt
2 tablespoons butter or margarine	1½ tablespoons butter or margarine
2 tablespoons honey	1½ tablespoons honey
1½ teaspoons Red Star brand active dry yeast for all machines except 1½-pound Welbilt/Dak machines (use 2 teaspoons yeast)	1½ teaspoons Red Star brand active dry yeast for all machines

Place all ingredients in bread pan, select Dough setting, and press Start.

When dough has risen long enough, the machine will beep. Turn off bread machine, remove bread pan, and turn out dough onto a floured countertop or cutting board. Gently roll and stretch dough into an 18-inch rope.

FOR 1½-POUND

Grease two 12-cup muffin tins. With a sharp knife, divide dough into 18 pieces. (Hint: First cut dough into 6 equal pieces, then cut each of those into 3 pieces.)

FOR 1-POUND

Grease one 12-cup muffin tin. With a sharp knife, divide dough into 12 pieces.

Place rolls in muffin tin(s). Cover and let rise in a warm oven 20 to 30 minutes until doubled. (Hint: To warm oven slightly, turn oven on Warm setting for 2 minutes, then turn it off, and place covered rolls in oven to rise. Remove tin from oven to preheat.)

Preheat oven to 400°F. Bake for 12 minutes until brown. Remove from oven and serve warm.

1½-pound dough yields 18 rolls
1-pound dough yields 12 rolls

MENU SELECTION: DOUGH

** OLD-FASHIONED OATMEAL ** ROLLS

These are best served warm, but Lois's neighbor, George, claims they're also great cold, split in half, and filled with thinly sliced turkey.

1½-POUND

1 cup old-fashioned rolled oats
1 cup milk (for Welbilt/Dak machines add 2 tablespoons more milk)
2 cups all-purpose flour
1 teaspoon salt
3 tablespoons butter or margarine
1 tablespoon sugar
1½ teaspoons Red Star brand active dry yeast for all machines except 1½-pound Welbilt/Dak machines (use 2 teaspoons yeast)
2 tablespoons melted butter or margarine

1-POUND

⅔ cup old-fashioned rolled oats
¾ cup milk (for Welbilt machine add 1 tablespoon more milk)
1⅓ cups all-purpose flour
½ teaspoon salt
2 tablespoons butter or margarine
2 teaspoons sugar
1½ teaspoons Red Star brand active dry yeast for all machines
2 tablespoons melted butter or margarine

Place all ingredients except melted butter in bread pan, select Dough setting, and press Start.

When dough has risen long enough, the machine will beep. Turn off bread machine, remove bread pan, and turn out dough onto a floured countertop or cutting board. Gently roll and stretch dough into an 18-inch rope.

FOR 1½-POUND

With a sharp knife, divide dough into 12 pieces.

FOR 1-POUND

With a sharp knife, divide dough into 8 pieces. Grease a large baking sheet. Shape each piece into a round ball; flatten slightly; place on cookie sheet. With a sharp knife, cut an X in the top of each roll. Cover and let rise in a warm oven 30 to 45 minutes until doubled. (Hint: To warm oven slightly, turn oven on Warm setting for 2 minutes, then turn it off, and place covered rolls in oven to rise. Remove sheet from oven to preheat.)

Preheat oven to 425°F. Brush each roll with melted butter. Bake for 12 to 15 minutes until brown. (Note: Rolls will flatten out slightly during baking.) Remove from oven and serve warm.

1½-pound dough yields 12 rolls
1-pound dough yields 8 rolls

MENU SELECTION: DOUGH

∙∙ BUTTERHORN ROLLS ∙∙

Make these rolls just once and they will become one of your favorites. They look impressive but they're deceptively simple to make because the dough is so easy to handle. They're rich, tender rolls—perfect for company dinners or festive holiday meals.

1½-POUND

¾ cup milk (for Welbilt/Dak
   machines add 2 tablespoons
   more milk)
1 egg
3 cups all-purpose flour
1 teaspoon salt
⅓ cup oil
⅓ cup sugar
1½ teaspoons Red Star brand
   active dry yeast for all
   machines except 1½-pound
   Welbilt/Dak machines (use 2
   teaspoons yeast)
1½ tablespoons melted butter
   or margarine

1-POUND

½ cup milk (for Welbilt machine
   add 1 tablespoon more milk)
1 egg
2 cups all-purpose flour
½ teaspoon salt
¼ cup oil
¼ cup sugar
1½ teaspoons Red Star brand
   active dry yeast for all
   machines
1 tablespoon melted butter or
   margarine

Place all ingredients except melted butter in bread pan, select Dough setting, and press Start.

When dough has risen long enough, the machine will beep. Turn off bread machine, remove bread pan, and turn out dough onto a floured countertop or cutting board. Shape dough into a log.

FOR 1½-POUND

With a sharp knife, divide dough into 3 pieces; roll each piece into a ball.

FOR 1-POUND

With a sharp knife, divide dough into 2 pieces; roll each piece into a ball.

With a rolling pin, roll each ball, one at a time, into a 9-inch circle. With a sharp knife or pizza cutter, divide each circle into 8 wedges, as if cutting a pizza. Starting at the wide end, roll up each wedge toward the point. Place rolls on an ungreased baking sheet, point side underneath. Cover and let rise in a warm oven 30 to 45 minutes until doubled. (Hint: To warm oven slightly, turn oven on Warm setting for 2 minutes, then turn it off, and place covered rolls in oven to rise. Remove sheet from oven to preheat.)

Preheat oven to 375°F. Brush rolls lightly with melted butter. Bake for 12 to 15 minutes until golden. Remove from oven and serve warm.

1½-pound dough yields 24 rolls
1-pound dough yields 16 rolls

MENU SELECTION: DOUGH

◆◆ GARLIC CHEESE ROLLS ◆◆

These garlicky rolls are incredibly light and delicious hot out of the oven! We've also found that they go over very well at potluck suppers.

1½-POUND

1 cup water (for Welbilt/Dak machines add 2 tablespoons more water)
3 cups all-purpose flour
1½ teaspoons salt
1½ tablespoons butter or margarine
3 tablespoons sugar
2 tablespoons nonfat dry milk powder
1½ teaspoons Red Star brand active dry yeast for all machines except 1½-pound Welbilt/Dak machines (use 2 teaspoons yeast)
¼ cup melted butter or margarine
1 clove garlic, crushed
2 tablespoons grated Parmesan cheese

1-POUND

¾ cup water (for Welbilt machine add 1 tablespoon more water)
2 cups all-purpose flour
1 teaspoon salt
1 tablespoon butter or margarine
2 tablespoons sugar
1 tablespoon nonfat dry milk powder
1½ teaspoons Red Star brand active dry yeast for all machines
¼ cup melted butter or margarine
1 clove garlic, crushed
2 tablespoons grated Parmesan cheese

Place first 7 ingredients in bread pan, select Dough setting, and press Start.

When dough has risen long enough, the machine will beep. Turn off bread machine, remove bread pan, and turn out dough onto a floured countertop or cutting board. Gently roll and stretch dough into a 24-inch rope. Grease two 8-inch pie pans.

FOR 1½-POUND

With a sharp knife, divide dough into 24 pieces. (Hint: First cut dough into 12 equal pieces, then cut each of those in half.)

FOR 1-POUND

With a sharp knife, divide dough into 16 pieces. (Hint: First cut dough into 8 equal pieces, then cut each of those in half.)

Shape into balls; place in prepared pie pans. In a small bowl, combine butter and garlic; pour over rolls. Sprinkle with Parmesan cheese.

Cover and let rise in warm oven 30 to 45 minutes until doubled. (Hint: To warm oven slightly, turn oven on Warm setting for 2 minutes, then turn it off, and place covered dough in oven to rise. Remove pan from oven to preheat.)

Preheat oven to 375°F. Bake for 15 minutes until golden. Remove from oven, cut apart, and serve warm.

1½-pound dough yields 24 rolls
1-pound dough yields 16 rolls

MENU SELECTION: DOUGH

✦✦ EGG BUNS ✦✦

This recipe produces a shiny, plump, eggy roll that would look beautiful in a big basket of assorted buns and rolls.

1½-POUND

⅝ cup milk (for Welbilt/Dak machines add 2 tablespoons more milk)

2 eggs

3 cups all-purpose flour

1½ teaspoons salt

⅓ cup butter or margarine

3 tablespoons sugar

1½ teaspoons Red Star brand active dry yeast for all machines except 1½-pound Welbilt/Dak machines (use 2 teaspoons yeast)

1 lightly beaten egg

1-POUND

¼ cup milk (for Welbilt machine add 1 tablespoon more milk)

2 eggs

2 cups all-purpose flour

1 teaspoon salt

¼ cup butter or margarine

2 tablespoons sugar

1½ teaspoons Red Star brand active dry yeast for all machines

1 lightly beaten egg

Place all ingredients except lightly beaten egg in bread pan, select Dough setting, and press Start.

When dough has risen long enough, the machine will beep. Turn off bread machine, remove bread pan, and turn out dough onto a floured countertop or cutting board.

FOR 1½-POUND

Gently roll and stretch dough into a 24-inch rope. With a sharp knife, divide dough into 28 pieces. (Hint: First cut dough into 7 equal pieces, then cut each of those into 4 small pieces.)

FOR 1-POUND

Gently roll and stretch dough into an 18-inch rope. With a sharp knife, divide dough into 18 pieces. (Hint: First cut dough into 6 equal pieces, then cut each of those into 3 pieces.)

Grease a large baking sheet. Roll each piece into a ball and place on sheet. Cover and let rise in a warm oven 30 to 45 minutes until doubled. (Hint: To warm oven slightly, turn oven on Warm setting for 2 minutes, then turn it off, and place covered dough in oven to rise. Remove sheet from oven to preheat.)

Preheat oven to 375°F. Brush rolls with beaten egg. Bake for 10 minutes until brown. Remove from oven. Serve either warm or cold.

1½-pound dough yields 28 buns
1-pound dough yields 18 buns

MENU SELECTION: DOUGH

⁓ CARAWAY RYE PAN ROLLS ⁓

These are rich, tender pan rolls—the perfect accompaniment to hearty split pea soup or a pork chop and sauerkraut supper.

1½-POUND	1-POUND
¾ cup water (for Welbilt/Dak machines add 2 tablespoons more water)	⅔ cup water (for Welbilt machine add 1 tablespoon more water)
½ cup sour cream	⅓ cup sour cream
2 cups all-purpose flour	1½ cups all-purpose flour
1 cup rye flour	¾ cup rye flour
2 teaspoons salt	1½ teaspoons salt
1 tablespoon sugar	2 teaspoons sugar
1 tablespoon caraway seeds	2 teaspoons caraway seeds
1½ teaspoons Red Star brand active dry yeast for all machines except 1½-pound Welbilt/Dak machines (use 2 teaspoons yeast)	1½ teaspoons Red Star brand active dry yeast for all machines

Place all ingredients in bread pan, select Dough setting, and press Start.

When dough has risen long enough, the machine will beep. Turn off bread machine, remove bread pan, and turn out dough onto a floured countertop or cutting board. (This is a very sticky dough, so keep your hands and the countertop well covered with flour.) Gently roll and stretch dough into an 18-inch rope.

FOR 1½-POUND

Grease a 9 × 13 × 2-inch pan. With a sharp knife, divide dough into 12 pieces; roll each into a ball and place in pan.

FOR 1-POUND

Grease a 9-inch round or square cake pan. With a sharp knife, divide dough into 9 pieces; roll each into a ball and place in pan.

Cover and let rise in a warm oven 30 to 45 minutes until doubled. (Hint: To warm oven slightly, turn oven on Warm setting for 2 minutes, then turn it off, and place covered dough in oven to rise. Remove pan from oven to preheat.)

Preheat oven to 400°F. Bake for 18 minutes until golden. Remove from oven and serve warm.

1½-pound dough yields 12 rolls
1-pound dough yields 9 rolls

MENU SELECTION: DOUGH

◆◆ SCANDINAVIAN RYE ROLLS ◆◆

You've probably never tasted a roll quite like this. It combines rye, orange, and a light anise flavor.

1½-POUND	1-POUND
½ cup milk	⅜ cup milk
½ cup water (for Welbilt/Dak machines add 2 tablespoons more water)	⅜ cup water (for Welbilt machine add 1 tablespoon more water)
1 cup rye flour	⅔ cup rye flour
2 cups all-purpose flour	1⅓ cups all-purpose flour
½ teaspoon salt	½ teaspoon salt
1 tablespoon butter or margarine	1 tablespoon butter or margarine
1 tablespoon molasses	2 teaspoons molasses
Grated rind of 1 orange	Grated rind of ½ orange
1 teaspoon fennel seeds	½ teaspoon fennel seeds
1½ teaspoons Red Star brand active dry yeast for all machines except 1½-pound Welbilt/Dak machines (use 2 teaspoons yeast)	1½ teaspoons Red Star brand active dry yeast for all machines

Place all ingredients in bread pan, select Dough setting, and press Start.

When dough has risen long enough, the machine will beep. Turn off bread machine, remove bread pan, and turn out dough onto a floured countertop or cutting board. Gently roll and stretch dough into a 24-inch rope.

FOR 1½-POUND

Grease a 9 × 13 × 2-inch pan. With a sharp knife, divide dough into 18 pieces. (Hint: First cut dough into 6 equal pieces, then cut each of those into 3 small pieces.) Shape into balls and place in pan.

FOR 1-POUND

Grease a 9-inch square cake pan. With a sharp knife, divide dough into 12 pieces. Shape into balls and place in pan.

Cover and let rise in a warm oven 30 to 45 minutes until doubled. (Hint: To warm oven slightly, turn oven on Warm setting for 2 minutes, then turn it off, and place covered rolls in oven to rise. Remove pan from oven to preheat.)

Preheat oven to 350°F. Bake for 20 to 25 minutes until golden. Remove from oven and serve warm.

1½-pound dough yields 18 rolls
1-pound dough yields 12 rolls

MENU SELECTION: DOUGH

•• BUCKWHEAT BISCUITS ••

These stout-hearted biscuits go well with a bowl of soup for lunch or just served warm with homemade apricot jam at breakfast.

<table>
<tr><td>

1½-POUND

1¼ cups buttermilk (or 5 tablespoons dry buttermilk powder and 1¼ cups water) (for Welbilt/Dak machines add 2 tablespoons more buttermilk)

3 cups all-purpose flour

¾ cup buckwheat flour

1½ teaspoons salt

2 tablespoons butter or margarine

1½ tablespoons molasses

1½ tablespoons sugar

¼ teaspoon baking soda

1½ teaspoons Red Star brand active dry yeast for all machines except 1½-pound Welbilt/Dak machines (use 2 teaspoons yeast)

3 tablespoons melted butter or margarine

</td><td>

1-POUND

1 cup buttermilk (or 4 tablespoons dry buttermilk powder and 1 cup water) (for Welbilt machine add 1 tablespoon more buttermilk)

2 cups all-purpose flour

½ cup buckwheat flour

1 teaspoon salt

1 tablespoon butter or margarine

1 tablespoon molasses

1 tablespoon sugar

¼ teaspoon baking soda

1½ teaspoons Red Star brand active dry yeast for all machines

2 tablespoons melted butter or margarine

</td></tr>
</table>

Place all ingredients except melted butter in bread pan, select Dough setting, and press Start.

When dough has risen long enough, the machine will beep. Turn off bread machine, remove bread pan, and turn out dough onto a floured countertop or cutting board.

With a rolling pin, roll dough to a 1-inch thickness. With a 2-inch biscuit cutter, cut out biscuits. Dip biscuits in melted butter; place on an ungreased cookie sheet. Let rise in warm oven 30 to 45 minutes until doubled. (Hint: To warm oven slightly, turn oven on Warm setting for 2 minutes, then turn it off, and place covered dough in oven to rise. Remove pan from oven to preheat.)

Preheat oven to 400°F. Bake for 15 minutes until brown. Remove from oven and serve warm.

1½-pound dough yields 20 to 22 biscuits
1-pound dough yields 14 to 16 biscuits

MENU SELECTION: DOUGH

◆◆ GARLIC AND HERB ◆◆
MONKEY BREAD

These are rich, tender rolls that will spice up any meal. They're perfect for a potluck or a buffet table because they don't require butter and they take up less space than a basket full of dinner rolls.

1½-POUND	1-POUND
½ cup water (for Welbilt/Dak machines add 2 tablespoons more water)	⅜ cup water (for Welbilt machine add 1 tablespoon more water)
½ cup sour cream	⅜ cup sour cream
3 cups all-purpose flour	2 cups all-purpose flour
1½ teaspoons salt	1 teaspoon salt
1½ tablespoons butter or margarine	1 tablespoon butter or margarine
3 tablespoons sugar	2 tablespoons sugar
1½ teaspoons Red Star brand active dry yeast for all machines except 1½-pound Welbilt/Dak machines (use 2 teaspoons yeast)	1½ teaspoons Red Star brand active dry yeast for all machines
4 tablespoons melted butter or margarine	3 tablespoons melted butter or margarine
2 cloves garlic, minced	1 clove garlic, minced
¼ teaspoon dried thyme	¼ teaspoon dried thyme
¼ teaspoon dried oregano	¼ teaspoon dried oregano
¼ teaspoon dried marjoram	¼ teaspoon dried marjoram

Place first 7 ingredients in bread pan, select Dough setting, and press Start.

When dough has risen long enough, the machine will beep. Turn off bread machine, remove bread pan, and turn out dough onto a floured countertop or cutting board. Gently roll and stretch dough into a 24-inch rope.

In a small bowl, combine melted butter, garlic, and herbs; set aside.

FOR 1½-POUND

With a sharp knife, divide dough into 40 small pieces. (Hint: First cut dough into 10 equal pieces, then cut each of those into 4 small pieces.) Butter a 9-inch ring mold or a 9 × 5 × 3-inch loaf pan.

FOR 1-POUND

With a sharp knife, divide dough into 30 small pieces. (Hint: First cut dough into 10 equal pieces, then cut each of those into 3 small pieces.) Butter an 8½ × 4½ × 2½-inch loaf pan.

Dip each piece into herb butter mixture and place in layers in the ring mold or loaf pans. Cover and let rise in a warm oven 30 to 45 minutes until doubled. (Hint: To warm oven slightly, turn oven on Warm setting for 2 minutes, then turn it off, and place covered rolls in oven to rise. Remove pan from oven to preheat.)

Preheat oven to 375°F. Bake for 15 to 20 minutes until brown. Turn out of pan onto a plate immediately, then invert onto a serving dish. Serve warm.

1½-pound dough yields 1 loaf
1-pound dough yields 1 loaf

MENU SELECTION: DOUGH

✦✦ ONION DILL PAN ROLLS ✦✦

For a rich, savory dinner roll, try these some night.

1½-POUND

⅔ cup water (for Welbilt/Dak machines add 2 tablespoons more water)
1 egg
3 cups all-purpose flour
1 teaspoon salt
1½ tablespoons butter or margarine
2 teaspoons sugar
⅔ cup cottage cheese
1 tablespoon dried minced onion
1 tablespoon dried dill
1½ teaspoons Red Star brand active dry yeast for all machines except 1½-pound Welbilt/Dak machines (use 2 teaspoons yeast)

1-POUND

⅜ cup water (for Welbilt machine add 1 tablespoon more water)
1 egg
2 cups all-purpose flour
1 teaspoon salt
1 tablespoon butter or margarine
1½ teaspoons sugar
½ cup cottage cheese
2 teaspoons dried minced onion
2 teaspoons dried dill
1½ teaspoons Red Star brand active dry yeast for all machines

Place all ingredients in bread pan, select Dough setting, and press Start.

When dough has risen long enough, the machine will beep. Turn off bread machine, remove bread pan, and turn out dough onto a floured countertop or cutting board. Gently roll and stretch dough into an 18-inch rope.

FOR 1½-POUND

Grease a 9 × 13 × 2-inch pan. With a sharp knife, divide dough into 12 pieces. Roll each piece into a ball; place in pan.

FOR 1-POUND

Grease a 9-inch square or round cake pan. With a sharp knife, divide dough into 9 pieces. Roll each piece into a ball; place in pan.

Cover and let rise in a warm oven 10 minutes. (Hint: To warm oven slightly, turn oven on Warm setting for 2 minutes, then turn it off, and place covered rolls in oven to rise. Remove pan from oven to preheat.)

Preheat oven to 350°F. Bake 25 to 30 minutes until lightly browned on top. Remove from oven, cut apart, and serve warm.

1½-pound dough yields 12 rolls
1-pound dough yields 9 rolls

MENU SELECTION: DOUGH

Sweet Rolls, Breads, and Coffee Cakes

◆◆ BASIC SWEET DOUGH ◆◆

This is a standard sweet dough that can be used in any recipe of your choice in this chapter.

1½-POUND

⅜ cup milk
⅜ cup water (for Welbilt/Dak machines add 2 tablespoons more water)
1 egg
3 cups all-purpose flour
1 teaspoon salt
4 tablespoons butter or margarine
⅓ cup sugar
1½ teaspoons Red Star brand active dry yeast for all machines except 1½-pound Welbilt/Dak machines (use 2 teaspoons yeast)

1-POUND

¼ cup milk
¼ cup water (for Welbilt machine add 1 tablespoon more water)
1 egg
2 cups all-purpose flour
1 teaspoon salt
3 tablespoons butter or margarine
¼ cup sugar
1½ teaspoons Red Star brand active dry yeast for all machines

Place all ingredients in bread pan, select Dough setting, and press Start.

When dough has risen long enough, the machine will beep. Turn off bread machine, remove bread pan, and turn out dough onto a floured countertop or cutting board.

Follow directions for specific recipe.

MENU SELECTION: DOUGH

122

••BASIC NOT-SO-SWEET DOUGH••

This dough is not quite as sweet and rich as the Basic Sweet Dough. It can be used in any recipe in this chapter.

1½-POUND

¾ cup water (for Welbilt/Dak machines add 2 tablespoons more water)

1 egg

3 cups all-purpose flour

1 teaspoon salt

3 tablespoons butter or margarine

2 tablespoons sugar

2 tablespoons nonfat dry milk powder

1½ teaspoons Red Star brand active dry yeast for all machines except 1½-pound Welbilt/Dak machines (use 2 teaspoons yeast)

1-POUND

½ cup water (for Welbilt machine add 1 tablespoon more water)

1 egg

2 cups all-purpose flour

1 teaspoon salt

2 tablespoons butter or margarine

1 tablespoon sugar

1 tablespoon nonfat dry milk powder

1½ teaspoons Red Star brand active dry yeast for all machines

Place all ingredients in bread pan, select Dough setting, and press Start.

When dough has risen long enough, the machine will beep. Turn off bread machine, remove bread pan, and turn out dough onto a floured countertop or cutting board.

Follow directions for specific recipe.

| MENU SELECTION: DOUGH |

·· BASIC BUTTERMILK ··
SWEET DOUGH

This is a rich sweet dough that can be used interchangeably with the other basic sweet doughs in this chapter.

1½-POUND

⅞ cup buttermilk (or 3
tablespoons dry buttermilk
powder and ⅞ cup water)
(for Welbilt/Dak machines add
2 tablespoons more
buttermilk)
1 egg
3 cups all-purpose flour
1 teaspoon salt
4 tablespoons butter or
margarine
¼ cup sugar
¼ teaspoon baking soda
1½ teaspoons Red Star brand
active dry yeast for all
machines except 1½-pound
Welbilt/Dak machines (use 2
teaspoons yeast)

1-POUND

⅝ cup buttermilk (or 2
tablespoons dry buttermilk
powder and ⅝ cup water)
(for Welbilt machine add 1
tablespoon more buttermilk)
1 egg
2 cups all-purpose flour
1 teaspoon salt
3 tablespoons butter or
margarine
3 tablespoons sugar
¼ teaspoon baking soda
1½ teaspoons Red Star brand
active dry yeast for all
machines

Place all ingredients in bread pan, select Dough setting, and press Start.

When dough has risen long enough, the machine will beep. Turn off bread machine, remove bread pan, and turn out dough onto a floured countertop or cutting board.

Follow directions for specific recipe.

MENU SELECTION: DOUGH

•• BASIC 100% WHOLE WHEAT •• SWEET DOUGH

If you prefer whole wheat doughs, this can be used in any recipe of your choice in this chapter.

1½-POUND

⅜ cup milk
⅜ cup water (for Welbilt/Dak machines add 2 tablespoons more water)
1 egg
3 cups whole wheat flour
1 teaspoon salt
4 tablespoons butter or margarine
¼ cup brown sugar
1½ teaspoons Red Star brand active dry yeast for all machines except 1½-pound Welbilt/Dak machines (use 2 teaspoons yeast)

1-POUND

¼ cup milk
¼ cup water (for Welbilt machine add 1 tablespoon more water)
1 egg
2 cups whole wheat flour
½ teaspoon salt
3 tablespoons butter or margarine
3 tablespoons brown sugar
1½ teaspoons Red Star brand active dry yeast for all machines

Place all ingredients in bread pan, select Dough setting, and press Start.

When dough has risen long enough, the machine will beep. Turn off bread machine, remove bread pan, and turn out dough onto a floured countertop or cutting board.

Follow directions for specific recipe.

MENU SELECTION: DOUGH

•• BASIC WHOLE WHEAT ••
SWEET DOUGH

The combination of whole-wheat and all-purpose flours make this a lighter version of the 100% whole-wheat sweet dough. Use it in your choice of recipes in this chapter.

1½-POUND

⅜ cup milk
⅜ cup water (for Welbilt/Dak machines add 2 tablespoons more water)
1 egg
1½ cups whole wheat flour
1½ cups all-purpose flour
1 teaspoon salt
4 tablespoons butter or margarine
¼ cup brown sugar
1½ teaspoons Red Star brand active dry yeast for all machines except 1½-pound Welbilt/Dak machines (use 2 teaspoons yeast)

1-POUND

¼ cup milk
¼ cup water (for Welbilt machine add 1 tablespoon more water)
1 egg
1 cup whole wheat flour
1 cup all-purpose flour
½ teaspoon salt
3 tablespoons butter or margarine
3 tablespoons brown sugar
1½ teaspoons Red Star brand active dry yeast for all machines

Place all ingredients in bread pan, select Dough setting, and press Start.

When dough has risen long enough, the machine will beep. Turn off bread machine, remove bread pan, and turn out dough onto a floured countertop or cutting board.

Follow directions for specific recipe.

MENU SELECTION: DOUGH

✦✦ COCONUT PECAN ROLLS ✦✦

These are easy to make and a big hit with friends—our favorite combination. The surprise ingredient is canned coconut pecan cake frosting!

1½-POUND	1-POUND
Dough	**Dough**
Sweet dough of your choice, such as Buttermilk Sweet Dough (page 124)	Sweet dough of your choice, such as Buttermilk Sweet Dough (page 124)
Topping	**Topping**
One 16-ounce can coconut pecan cake frosting ½ cup chopped pecans	1 cup canned coconut pecan cake frosting ⅓ cup chopped pecans

Place dough ingredients in bread pan, select Dough setting, and press Start.

When dough has risen long enough, the machine will beep. Turn off bread machine, remove bread pan, and turn out dough onto a floured countertop or cutting board. Gently roll and stretch dough into a 20-inch rope.

FOR 1½-POUND

Spread frosting on bottom of a $9 \times 13 \times 2$-inch pan or two round 8- or 9-inch cake pans; sprinkle pecans evenly on top. With a sharp knife, divide dough into 12 pieces.

FOR 1-POUND

Spread frosting on bottom of an 8- or 9-inch round cake pan; sprinkle pecans evenly on top. With a sharp knife, divide dough into 9 pieces.

Roll each piece of dough into a ball and place in prepared pan(s). Cover and let rise in a warm oven 30 to 45 minutes until doubled. (Hint: To warm oven slightly, turn oven on Warm setting for 2 minutes, then turn it off, and place covered dough in oven to rise. Remove pan(s) from oven to preheat.)

Preheat oven to 350°F. Bake for 25 to 30 minutes until brown. Remove from oven, invert onto serving dish. Serve warm.

1½-pound dough yields 12 rolls
1-pound dough yields 9 rolls

MENU SELECTION: DOUGH

▪▪ *JIM'S CINNAMON ROLLS* ▪▪

Nothing can top the aroma and warm, sweet stickiness of cinnamon rolls, fresh from the oven. What you'll also love about these luscious, light rolls is that the machine does half the work; they're no longer a major production. The first time Lois made these, her husband Jim emphatically declared them his favorite recipe of all—high praise from one who had been completely noncommittal about the breads until then!

1½-POUND

Dough

Sweet dough of your choice, such as Basic Sweet Dough (page 122)

Glaze

5 tablespoons melted butter or margarine
½ cup brown sugar

Filling

1 tablespoon melted butter or margarine
2 tablespoons granulated sugar
1 tablespoon ground cinnamon
2 tablespoons brown sugar
½ cup raisins (optional)

1-POUND

Dough

Sweet dough of your choice, such as Basic Sweet Dough (page 122)

Glaze

3 tablespoons melted butter or margarine
⅓ cup brown sugar

Filling

1 tablespoon melted butter or margarine
1 tablespoons granulated sugar
1½ teaspoons ground cinnamon
1 tablespoon brown sugar
⅓ cup raisins (optional)

Place dough ingredients in bread pan, select Dough setting, and press Start.

When dough has risen long enough, the machine will beep. Turn off bread machine, remove bread pan, and turn out dough onto a floured countertop or cutting board.

FOR 1½-POUND

Pour the melted butter for the glaze into one $9 \times 13 \times 2$-inch pan or two 8- or 9-inch round cake pans; sprinkle with brown sugar. With a rolling pin, roll dough into a 9×18-inch rectangle.

FOR 1-POUND

Pour the melted butter for the glaze into one 9-inch round or square cake pan; sprinkle with brown sugar. With a rolling pin, roll dough into an 8×14-inch rectangle.

For the filling, brush the melted butter on the dough. In a small bowl, combine the granulated sugar, cinnamon, brown sugar, and raisins; sprinkle over dough. Starting with long edge, roll up dough; pinch seams to seal. With a knife, lightly mark roll into 1½-inch sections. Slide a 12-inch piece of dental floss or heavy thread underneath. By bringing the ends of the floss up and crisscrossing them at the top of each mark, you can cut through the roll by pulling the strings in opposite directions. Place rolls cut side up in prepared pan(s), flattening them slightly.* Cover and let rise in a warm oven 30 to 45 minutes until doubled. (Hint: To warm oven slightly, turn oven on Warm setting for 2 minutes, then turn it off, and place covered dough in oven to rise. Remove pan(s) from oven to preheat.)

Preheat oven to 350°F. Bake 25 to 30 minutes until golden brown. Remove from oven and immediately invert rolls onto a large platter or serving dish. Serve warm.

1½-pound dough yields 12 rolls
1-pound dough yields 9 rolls

MENU SELECTION: DOUGH

*The rolls can be covered with foil at this point and refrigerated overnight or frozen for 1 month. Before baking, allow rolls to thaw completely and rise in a warm oven 30 minutes. (Hint: On a moment's notice you can have a fabulous gift on hand by placing uncooked rolls in disposable cake pans, covering them with foil, attaching a label with thawing and baking directions to the top, and then freezing them.)

⁕⁕ MINI CINNAMON ROLLS ⁕⁕

These cinnamon rolls are the perfect addition to a buffet brunch; they're just the right size and there are plenty to go around.

1½-POUND	1-POUND
Dough	**Dough**
Sweet dough of your choice, such as Basic Not-So-Sweet Dough (page 123)	Sweet dough of your choice, such as Basic Not-So-Sweet Dough (page 123)
Filling	**Filling**
3 tablespoons melted butter or margarine	2 tablespoons melted butter or margarine
⅓ cup sugar	¼ cup sugar
2 teaspoons ground cinnamon	1½ teaspoons ground cinnamon
Icing	**Icing**
1 cup confectioners' sugar	½ cup confectioners' sugar
3 to 4 teaspoons milk or cream	1½ to 2 teaspoons milk or cream
½ teaspoon vanilla extract	¼ teaspoon vanilla extract

Place dough ingredients in bread pan, select Dough setting, and press Start.

When dough has risen long enough, the machine will beep. Turn off bread machine, remove bread pan, and turn out dough onto a floured countertop or cutting board. Shape dough into a log.

FOR 1½-POUND

Brush two 9-inch cake pans with a little of the melted butter for the filling. With a sharp knife, divide dough in half. With a rolling pin, roll each piece into a 20×5-inch rectangle.

FOR 1-POUND

Brush one 9-inch cake pan with a little of the melted butter for the filling. With a rolling pin, roll dough into one 20×8-inch rectangle.

For the filling, brush each rectangle of dough with the rest of the melted butter. In a small bowl, combine the sugar and cinnamon; sprinkle mixture over dough. Starting with the long edge, roll up dough tightly; pinch seam to seal. With a knife, lightly mark each roll into 24 pieces. Slide a 12-inch piece of dental floss or heavy thread underneath. By bringing the ends of the floss up and crisscrossing them at the top of each mark, you can cut through the roll by pulling the strings in opposite directions. Place the rolls cut side up in prepared pans.* Cover and let rise in a warm oven 30 to 45 minutes until doubled. (Hint: To warm oven slightly, turn oven on Warm setting for 2 minutes, then turn it off, and place covered dough in oven to rise.)

Preheat oven to 350°F. Bake for 20 to 25 minutes until brown. Remove from oven, turn out onto plate(s), then invert onto serving dishes. Allow rolls to cool slightly.

Meanwhile, in a small bowl, combine the confectioners' sugar, milk or cream, and vanilla for the icing, using enough milk or cream to make the icing thin enough to drizzle on the rolls. Once the rolls have cooled slightly, drizzle with icing and serve.

1½-pound dough yields 48 rolls
1-pound dough yields 24 rolls

MENU SELECTION: DOUGH

*The rolls can be covered with foil at this point and refrigerated overnight or frozen for up to one month. Before baking, allow rolls to thaw completely and rise in a warm oven 30 minutes.

♦♦ CARAMEL STICKY BUNS ♦♦

These rolls bake in a thick, syrupy sea of sugar. They'll appeal only to the truly serious sweet treat lover—a person who can eat brown sugar straight from the box. These buns should be eaten fresh out of the oven because they really don't keep well.

1½-POUND	1-POUND
Dough	**Dough**
Sweet dough of your choice, such as Basic Sweet Dough (page 122)	Sweet dough of your choice, such as Basic Sweet Dough (page 122)
Topping	**Topping**
2 tablespoons melted butter or margarine	2 tablespoons melted butter or margarine
¾ cup brown sugar	½ cup brown sugar
⅜ cup light or dark corn syrup	¼ cup light or dark corn syrup
Filling	**Filling**
1 tablespoon melted butter or margarine	1 tablespoon melted butter or margarine
⅓ cup brown sugar	¼ cup brown sugar
1 teaspoon ground cinnamon	1 teaspoon ground cinnamon
⅓ cup raisins	¼ cup raisins

Place dough ingredients in bread pan, select Dough setting, and press Start.

When dough has risen long enough, the machine will beep. Turn off bread machine, remove bread pan, and turn out dough onto a floured countertop or cutting board.

FOR 1½-POUND

Brush one 9 × 13 × 2-inch pan or two 9-inch round or square cake pans with 1 tablespoon melted butter for topping. Sprinkle the brown sugar over the bottom of the pan(s). Pour corn syrup over the sugar. With a rolling pin, roll dough into an 18 × 10-inch rectangle.

FOR 1-POUND

Brush a 9-inch round or square cake pan with 1 tablespoon melted butter for topping. Sprinkle the brown sugar over the bottom of the pan. Pour corn syrup over the sugar. With a rolling pin, roll dough into 12 × 10-inch rectangle.

For the filling, brush dough with 1 tablespoon melted butter. In a small bowl, combine the brown sugar, cinnamon, and raisins; sprinkle over dough. Starting with the long edge, roll up dough; pinch seam to seal. With roll seam side down, lightly mark it into 1-inch sections with a knife. Slide a 12-inch piece of dental floss or heavy thread underneath. By bringing the ends of

132

the floss up and crisscrossing them at the top of each mark, you can cut through the roll by pulling the strings in opposite directions. Place rolls cut side up in prepared pan(s). Brush rolls with remaining 1 tablespoon melted butter. Cover and let rise in a warm oven 30 to 45 minutes until doubled. (Hint: To warm oven slightly, turn oven on Warm setting for 2 minutes, then turn it off, and place covered dough in oven to rise. Remove pan(s) from oven to preheat.)

Preheat oven to 325°F. Bake about 45 minutes until brown. Remove from oven and invert onto a serving platter. Leave pan on top of rolls 1 to 2 minutes, allowing topping to drip out of pan. Serve warm. (They do not keep well.)

1½-pound dough yields 18 rolls
1-pound dough yields 12 rolls

| MENU SELECTION: DOUGH |

✦✦ ORANGE COCONUT ✦✦
SWEET ROLLS

The orange and coconut combine to make these exotic rolls memorable.
Serve proudly to guests.

| 1½-POUND | 1-POUND |

Dough

*Sweet dough of your choice,
    such as Buttermilk Sweet
    Dough (page 124)*

Dough

*Sweet dough of your choice,
    such as Buttermilk Sweet
    Dough (page 124)*

Filling

*1 cup flaked coconut
½ cup granulated sugar
Grated rind of 3 oranges
2 tablespoons melted butter or
    margarine*

Filling

*½ cup flaked coconut
¼ cup granulated sugar
Grated rind of 2 oranges
1 tablespoon melted butter or
    margarine*

Icing

*1 cup confectioners' sugar
3 to 4 teaspoons orange juice*

Icing

*½ cup confectioners' sugar
1 to 2 teaspoons orange juice*

Place dough ingredients in bread pan, select Dough setting, and press Start.

When dough has risen long enough, the machine will beep. Turn off bread machine, remove bread pan, and turn out dough onto a floured countertop or cutting board.

In a small bowl, combine the coconut, granulated sugar, and grated orange rind for the filling; set aside.

FOR 1½-POUND

Grease two 9-inch round cake pans. With a sharp knife, divide dough in half; with a rolling pin, roll each piece into a 12 × 8-inch rectangle.

FOR 1-POUND

Grease one 9-inch round cake pan. With a rolling pin, roll the dough into a 12 × 8-inch rectangle.

For the filling, brush each rectangle with 1 tablespoon of the melted butter; sprinkle filling mixture evenly on top. Starting with the long edge, roll up dough; pinch seam to seal. With the seam side down, lightly mark the roll into 1-inch sections with a knife. Slide a 12-inch piece of dental floss or heavy thread underneath. By bringing the ends of the floss up and crisscrossing them at the top of each mark, you can cut through the roll by pulling the strings in opposite directions. Place rolls cut side up in prepared pan(s). Cover and let rise in warm oven 30 to 45 minutes until doubled. (Hint: To warm oven slightly, turn oven on Warm setting for 2 minutes, then turn it off, and place covered rolls in oven to rise. Remove pan(s) from oven to preheat.)

Preheat oven to 350°F. Bake for 30 minutes until golden. Remove from oven, turn out onto a plate, and then invert onto a serving dish. Allow rolls to cool slightly. Meanwhile, in a small bowl, combine the sugar and orange juice for the icing, adding enough orange juice to make the icing thin enough to drizzle. When rolls have cooled slightly, drizzle icing on top. Serve warm.

1½-pound dough yields 24 rolls
1-pound dough yields 12 rolls

MENU SELECTION: DOUGH

◆◆ GOOEY ORANGE ROLLS ◆◆

As their name implies, these rolls have a piquant citrus flavor and a bubbly orange sauce. They make an out-of-the-ordinary Sunday brunch treat, one worth repeating for a whole month of Sundays!

1½-POUND	1-POUND

Dough

Sweet dough of your choice,
   such as Basic Sweet Dough
   (page 122)

Topping

1 (6-ounce) can frozen orange
   juice concentrate
½ cup sugar
4 tablespoons butter or
   margarine
Grated rind of ½ orange

Filling

¼ cup sugar
1 teaspoon ground cinnamon
⅛ teaspoon ground cloves
Grated rind of ½ orange

Dough

Sweet dough of your choice,
   such as Basic Sweet Dough
   (page 122)

Topping

1 (6-ounce) can frozen orange
   juice concentrate
½ cup sugar
4 tablespoons butter or
   margarine
Grated rind of ½ orange

Filling

3 tablespoons sugar
¾ teaspoon ground cinnamon
Pinch of ground cloves
Grated rind of ½ orange

Place dough ingredients in bread pan, select Dough setting, and press Start.

When dough has risen long enough, the machine will beep. Turn off bread machine, remove bread pan, and turn out dough onto a floured countertop or cutting board.

For the topping, in a small saucepan, combine the orange juice and sugar. Cook on medium heat until sugar dissolves. Add butter and grated orange rind; stir.

FOR 1½-POUND

Pour the topping into a 9 × 13 × 2-inch pan. With a rolling pin, roll dough into a 12-inch square.

FOR 1-POUND

Pour the topping into a 9-inch square or round cake pan. With a rolling pin, roll dough into a 9-inch square.

For the filling, in a small bowl, combine the sugar, cinnamon, cloves, and grated orange rind; sprinkle evenly on dough. Starting at one edge, roll up dough; pinch seam to seal. With roll seam side down, lightly mark the dough into 1-inch sections with a knife. Slide a 12-inch piece of dental floss or heavy thread underneath. By bringing the ends of the floss up and crisscrossing them at the top of each mark, you can cut through the roll by pulling the strings in opposite directions. Place rolls cut side up in prepared pan. Cover and let rise in a warm oven 30 to 45 minutes until doubled. (Hint: To warm oven slightly, turn oven on Warm setting for 2 minutes, then turn it off, and place covered rolls in oven to rise. Remove pan from oven to preheat.)

Preheat oven to 400°F. Bake for 15 to 20 minutes until brown. Remove from oven and immediately invert pan onto a serving platter. Serve warm.

$1\frac{1}{2}$-pound dough yields 12 rolls
1-pound dough yields 9 rolls

| MENU SELECTION: DOUGH |

⋆⋆ CINNAMON BUBBLE ⋆⋆
COFFEE CAKE

We love this cinnamon-sugar extravagance hot out of the oven, served with a cup of freshly brewed coffee—it's the perfect way to start a weekend!

1½-POUND	1-POUND
Dough	**Dough**
Sweet dough of your choice, such as Basic Not-So-Sweet Dough (page 123)	Sweet dough of your choice, such as Basic Not-So-Sweet Dough (page 123)
Topping	**Topping**
¼ cup melted butter or margarine	¼ cup melted butter or margarine
¾ cup brown sugar	¾ cup brown sugar
1 teaspoon ground cinnamon	1 teaspoon ground cinnamon

Place dough ingredients in bread pan, select Dough setting, and press Start.

When dough has risen long enough, the machine will beep. Turn off bread machine, remove bread pan, and turn out dough onto a floured countertop or cutting board.

FOR 1½-POUND

Brush a 9-inch ring mold with a little of the melted butter needed for the topping. Gently roll and stretch dough into a 24-inch rope. With a sharp knife, divide dough into 60 pieces and roll each piece into a ball. (Hint: First cut dough into 12 equal pieces, then cut each of those into 5 small pieces.)

FOR 1-POUND

Brush an 8½ × 4½ × 2½-inch loaf pan with a little of the melted butter needed for the topping. Gently roll and stretch dough into a 20-inch rope. With a sharp knife, divide dough into 40 pieces and roll each piece into a ball. (Hint: First cut dough into 10 equal pieces, then cut each of those into 4 small pieces.)

In a small bowl, combine the brown sugar and cinnamon; sprinkle ¼ cup of sugar mixture into prepared pan. Dip each piece of dough into melted butter, then roll it in the remaining sugar mixture. Place sugar-coated pieces in pan in layers. Cover and let rise in warm oven 30 to 45 minutes until doubled. (Hint: To warm oven slightly, turn oven on Warm setting for 2 minutes, then turn it off, and place covered dough in oven to rise. Remove pan from oven to preheat.)

Preheat oven to 350°F. Bake for 25 to 30 minutes until brown. Remove from oven, turn out onto a plate, then invert onto serving dish. Serve warm.

1½-pound dough yields one 9-inch round coffee cake
1-pound dough yields one 8 × 4-inch loaf

MENU SELECTION: DOUGH

✦✦ ORANGE BUBBLE LOAF ✦✦

Serve this at a holiday brunch or on Christmas morning for a sure-fire crowd pleaser. To eat, pull away the sugary, orange-crusted rounds of dough from this attractive coffee cake.

1½-POUND	1-POUND
Dough	**Dough**
Sweet dough of your choice, such as Basic Sweet Dough (page 122)	Sweet dough of your choice, such as Basic Sweet Dough (page 122)
Grated rind of ½ lemon	Grated rind of ½ lemon
Glaze	**Glaze**
¼ cup melted butter or margarine	¼ cup melted butter or margarine
½ cup sugar	½ cup sugar
Grated rind of 2 oranges	Grated rind of 2 oranges

Place dough ingredients in bread pan, select Dough setting, and press Start.

When dough has risen long enough, the machine will beep. Turn off bread machine, remove bread pan, and turn out dough onto a floured countertop or cutting board.

FOR 1½-POUND

Brush a 10-inch ring mold with some of the melted butter needed for the glaze.

FOR 1-POUND

Brush an 8½ × 4½ × 2½-inch loaf pan with some of the melted butter needed for the glaze.

In a small bowl, combine remaining melted butter, sugar, and grated orange rind for the glaze. Pinch off small pieces of dough about the size of an acorn, and roll into balls. Roll each in the glaze and then place in prepared pan. Cover, and let rise in warm oven 30 to 45 minutes until doubled. (Hint: To warm oven slightly, turn oven on Warm setting for 2 minutes, then turn it off, and place covered dough in oven to rise. Remove pan from oven to preheat.)

Preheat oven to 350°F. Bake for 30 minutes until golden. Remove from oven, turn out onto a plate, and then invert onto serving plate. Serve warm.

1½-pound dough yields one 10-inch round coffee cake
1-pound dough yields one 8 × 4-inch loaf

MENU SELECTION: DOUGH

•• WHOLE WHEAT FRUIT ROLL ••

A strong whole wheat flavor makes this coffee cake different and surprising. If you omit the icing and use fruit-sweetened (sugarless) preserves, this coffee cake will fall into the "great taste, no guilt" category.

1½-POUND

Dough

Whole-wheat sweet dough of
  your choice, such as Basic
  100% Whole-Wheat Sweet
  Dough (page 125)

Filling

1½ cups any flavor fruit
  preserves

Icing

½ cup sifted confectioners'
  sugar
about 2½ teaspoons milk

1-POUND

Dough

Whole-wheat sweet dough of
  your choice, such as Basic
  100% Whole-Wheat Sweet
  Dough (page 125)

Filling

1 cup any flavor fruit preserves

Icing

½ cup sifted confectioners'
  sugar
about 2½ teaspoons milk

Place dough ingredients in bread pan, select Dough setting, and press Start.

When dough has risen long enough, the machine will beep. Turn off bread machine, remove bread pan, and turn out dough onto a floured countertop or cutting board.

FOR 1½-POUND

With a rolling pin, roll dough into a 10 × 14-inch rectangle.

FOR 1-POUND

With a rolling pin, roll dough into an 8 × 12-inch rectangle.

Grease a 10 × 15 × 1-inch jelly-roll pan or baking sheet with edges (to prevent spillage during baking). With a knife, lightly score the dough lengthwise, dividing it into thirds. Spread the preserves lengthwise down the center third of the dough. With a sharp knife, cut strips at 1-inch intervals down each side of the dough, from the edge to the filling. Alternately, cross the strips over the filling. Cover and let rise in a warm oven for 1 hour. (Hint: To warm oven slightly, turn oven on Warm setting for 2 minutes, then turn it off, and place the covered dough in the oven to rise. Remove pan from oven to preheat.)

Preheat oven to 350°F. Bake for 25 minutes. Remove from oven, place on a serving plate, and allow to cool slightly. Meanwhile in a small bowl, combine the confectioners' sugar and milk for the icing, adding enough milk to make the icing thin enough to drizzle on the coffee cake. Once the coffee cake has cooled slightly, drizzle icing on top and serve.

MENU SELECTION: DOUGH

•• AUNT CELIA'S RASPBERRY- •• CREAM COFFEE CAKE WITH ALMONDS

Every year, Linda's Aunt Celia makes an award-winning raspberry jam that's well worth a twelve-month wait. Of course, its goodness is enhanced with memories of many happy family breakfasts at her table. Thoughts of those times and that special jam inspired this coffee cake, which rates all the superlatives—simply scrumptious, incredibly edible, and outrageously delicious!

1½-POUND

Dough

¾ cup water (for Welbilt/Dak
    machines add 2 tablespoons
    more water)
1 egg
3 cups all-purpose flour
½ teaspoon salt
⅔ cup butter or margarine,
    softened
2 tablespoons sugar
1½ teaspoons Red Star brand
    active dry yeast for all
    machines except 1½-pound
    Welbilt/Dak machines (use 2
    teaspoons yeast)

Filling

5 tablespoons raspberry jam
1 (8-ounce) and 1 (3-ounce)
    package cream cheese,
    softened
1 egg
⅔ cup sugar

Topping

⅓ cup sliced almonds
1½ tablespoons sugar

1-POUND

Dough

½ cup water (for Welbilt
    machine add 1 tablespoon
    more water)
1 egg
2 cups all-purpose flour
¼ teaspoon salt
½ cup butter or margarine,
    softened
1 tablespoon sugar
1½ teaspoons Red Star brand
    active dry yeast for all
    machines

Filling

3 tablespoons raspberry jam
1 (8-ounce) package cream
    cheese, softened
1 egg
½ cup sugar

Topping

¼ cup sliced almonds
1 tablespoon sugar

141

Place dough ingredients in bread pan, select Dough setting, and press Start.

When dough has risen long enough, the machine will beep. Turn off bread machine, remove bread pan, and turn out dough onto a floured countertop or cutting board.

FOR 1½-POUND

With a sharp knife, divide dough in half. With a rolling pin, roll each half into a 9 × 13-inch rectangle. Gently place one of the rectangles in an ungreased 9 × 13 × 2-inch pan.

FOR 1-POUND

With a sharp knife, divide dough in half. With a rolling pin, roll each hallf into a 9-inch square. Gently place one of the squares in an ungreased 9-inch square pan.

Spread raspberry jam over dough in the pan. In a medium bowl, combine the cream cheese, egg, and sugar; beat with an electric mixer until well blended. With a spatula, carefully spread cream cheese mixture over the layer of jam. Place the other piece of dough on top of the cream cheese layer. Sprinkle the almonds and sugar over all. Cover and let rise in a warm oven 20 to 30 minutes until almost doubled. (Hint: To warm oven slightly, turn oven on Warm setting for 2 minutes, then turn it off, and place covered dough in oven to rise. Remove pan from oven to preheat.)

Preheat oven to 350°F. Bake 40 to 45 minutes until the filling has set. Remove from oven; serve warm or allow to cool slightly and serve at room temperature.

1½-pound dough yields one 9 × 13-inch coffee cake
1-pound dough yields one 9-inch square coffee cake

MENU SELECTION: DOUGH

142

◆◆ APPLE STRUDEL ◆◆

This recipe is easier than it looks and well worth a try.

1½-POUND

Dough

½ cup milk (for Welbilt/Dak
   machines add 2 tablespoons
   more milk)
2 eggs
3 cups all-purpose flour
1 teaspoon salt
¾ cup butter or margarine
⅓ cup granulated sugar
1½ teapoons Red Star brand
   active dry yeast for all
   machines except 1½-pound
   Welbilt/Dak machines (use 2
   teaspoons yeast)

Filling

2 tablespoons melted butter or
   margarine
3 cups peeled, cored, thinly
   sliced Granny Smith apples
1½ tablespoons all-purpose
   flour
½ cup raisins
½ cup brown sugar
1 teaspoon ground cinnamon

Icing

½ cup confectioners' sugar
about 2½ teaspoons milk

1-POUND

Dough

½ cup milk (for Welbilt machine
   add 1 tablespoon more milk)
1 egg
2 cups all-purpose flour
½ teaspoon salt
½ cup butter or margarine
¼ cup granulated sugar
1½ teaspoons Red Star brand
   active dry yeast for all
   machines

Filling

2 tablespoons melted butter or
   margarine
2 cups peeled, cored, thinly
   sliced Granny Smith apples
1 tablespoon all-purpose or
   unbleached flour
⅓ cup raisins
⅓ cup brown sugar
1 teaspoon ground cinnamon

Icing

⅓ cup confectioners' sugar
about 2 teaspoons milk

Place dough ingredients in bread pan, select Dough setting, and press Start.

When dough has risen long enough, the machine will beep. Turn off bread machine, remove bread pan, and turn out dough onto a heavily floured countertop or cutting board.

FOR 1½-POUND

With a rolling pin, roll dough into one large 20 × 12-inch rectangle or two 10 × 12-inch rectangles.

FOR 1-POUND

With a rolling pin, roll dough into one large 16 × 10-inch rectangle or two 8 × 10-inch rectangles.

Butter a 10 × 15 × 1-inch jelly-roll pan or a large baking sheet with edges (to avoid spillage during baking). Spread dough first with the melted butter and then with the apples, flour, raisins, brown sugar, and cinnamon. Starting from the long edge, carefully roll up dough; pinch edges and ends to seal. Place roll(s) seam side down on prepared pan. Shape roll(s) into large crescent(s) by curving ends slightly toward each other. Cover and let rise in warm oven about 45 minutes until doubled. (Hint: To warm oven slightly, turn oven on Warm setting for 2 minutes, then turn it off, and place covered dough in oven to rise. Remove pan from oven to preheat.)

Preheat oven to 350°F. Bake for 35 to 40 minutes until brown. Remove from oven and place on rack to cool.

In a small bowl, combine confectioners' sugar and milk for the icing, adding enough milk to make the icing thin enough to drizzle on the strudel. Once the strudel has cooled, drizzle icing on top and serve.

1½-pound dough yields 1 large or 2 small strudels
1-pound dough yields 1 large or 2 small strudels

MENU SELECTION: DOUGH

✦✦ IRENE'S BAVARIAN ✦✦
COFFEE CAKE

Our friend Irene thought this was the best of all the breads and coffee cakes we asked co-workers to taste-test. Once you make it, you'll understand why. Not only is it velvety rich and spicy, this coffee cake is amazingly quick and easy to create. We think it could also be served for dessert following a light meal.

1½-POUND	1-POUND
Dough	**Dough**
Sweet dough of your choice, such as Basic Sweet Dough (page 122)	Sweet dough of your choice, such as Basic Sweet Dough (page 122)
Topping	**Topping**
⅓ cup sugar	¼ cup sugar
1 teaspoon ground cinnamon	¾ teaspoon ground cinnamon
1 cup heavy cream	⅔ cup heavy cream

Place dough ingredients in bread pan, select Dough setting, and press Start.

When dough has risen long enough, the machine will beep. Turn off bread machine, remove bread pan, and turn out dough onto a floured countertop or cutting board.

FOR 1½-POUND

Grease a 9 × 13 × 2-inch pan. With a rolling pin, roll dough into a 9 × 13-inch rectangle.

FOR 1-POUND

Grease a 9-inch round or square cake pan. With a rolling pin, roll dough into a 9-inch square or circle, depending on the pan you're using.

Place dough in prepared pan. Cover and let rise in warm oven 30 to 45 minutes until doubled. (Hint: To warm oven slightly, turn oven on Warm setting for 2 minutes, then turn it off, and place covered dough in oven to rise. Remove pan from oven to preheat.)

With 2 fingers, punch deep holes all over the dough. In a small bowl, combine sugar and cinnamon; sprinkle mixture over dough. Drizzle cream evenly on top.

Preheat oven to 350°F. Bake for 25 to 30 minutes until the dough is thoroughly baked. Remove from the oven and serve warm.

1½-pound dough yields one 9 × 13-inch coffee cake
1-pound dough yields one 9-inch round or square coffee cake

MENU SELECTION: DOUGH

❖❖ AUNT BERTHA'S MORAVIAN ❖❖
SUGAR CAKE

This is a treat from the "old country." When Linda took this coffee cake to work one day to share at break, Janet, a co-worker, took one bite and exclaimed, "It's Aunt Bertha's coffee cake!" She was thrilled because it brought back fond memories of a long-lost family recipe. It seemed only fitting to name this in honor of Janet's Aunt Bertha.

1½-POUND

Dough

½ cup instant potato flakes
⅝ cup water (for Welbilt/Dak machines add 2 tablespoons more water)
2 eggs
3 cups all-purpose flour
1 teaspoon salt
½ cup butter or margarine
½ cup granulated sugar
1 teaspoon vanilla extract
2 teaspoons Red Star brand active dry yeast for all machines

Topping

1 cup light brown sugar
2 teaspoons ground cinnamon
½ cup melted butter or margarine

Icing

¾ cup confectioners' sugar
About 4 teaspoons milk

1-POUND

Dough

⅓ cup instant potato flakes
⅝ cup water (for Welbilt machine add 1 tablespoon more water)
1 egg
2 cups all-purpose flour
½ teaspoon salt
⅓ cup butter or margarine
⅓ cup granulated sugar
½ teaspoon vanilla extract
2 teaspoons Red Star brand active dry yeast for all machines

Topping

⅔ cup light brown sugar
1½ teaspoons ground cinnamon
⅓ cup melted butter or margarine

Icing

½ cup confectioners' sugar
About 3 teaspoons milk

Place dough ingredients in bread pan, select Dough setting, and press Start.

When dough has risen long enough, the machine will beep. Turn off bread machine, remove bread pan, and turn out dough onto a floured countertop or cutting board.

FOR 1½-POUND

Grease a $15 \times 10 \times 1$-inch jelly-roll pan or a $16 \times 12 \times 1$-inch baking pan.

FOR 1-POUND

Grease a $9 \times 13 \times 2$-inch pan.

Place dough in pan; gently stretching it, press it evenly into the pan. Cover and let rise in warm oven 30 to 45 minutes until doubled. (Hint: To warm oven slightly, turn oven on Warm setting for 2 minutes, then turn it off, and place covered dough in oven to rise. Remove pan from oven to preheat.)

In a small bowl, combine brown sugar and cinnamon for the topping. With 2 fingers, poke deep holes all over the dough. Sprinkle sugar mixture evenly over dough. Drizzle melted butter on top.

Preheat oven to 350°F. Bake for 20 to 25 minutes until golden brown. Remove from oven, place on a serving plate. Serve warm without icing or allow coffee cake to cool slightly, combine the confectioners' sugar and milk for the icing and drizzle on top of cooled coffee cake.

MENU SELECTION: DOUGH

✦✦ PORTUGUESE SWEET BREAD ✦✦

This is a very sweet coffee cake bread with a hint of lemon. It is delightful with afternoon tea.

1½-POUND LOAF

3 tablespoons instant potato
  flakes
¼ cup sweetened condensed
  milk
½ cup water (for Welbilt/Dak
  machines add 2 tablespoons
  more water)
½ teaspoon vanilla extract
¼ teaspoon lemon extract or
  grated rind of 1 lemon
2 eggs
3 cups bread flour
1 teaspoon salt
4 tablespoons butter or
  margarine
⅓ cup sugar
Pinch of ground nutmeg
3 teapoons Red Star brand
  active dry yeast for all
  machines
1 egg white, lightly beaten

1-POUND LOAF

2 tablespoons instant potato
  flakes
3 tablespoons sweetened
  condensed milk
⅓ cup water (for Welbilt
  machine add 1 tablespoon
  more water)
½ teaspoon vanilla extract
⅛ teaspoon lemon extract or
  grated rind of ½ lemon
1 egg
2 cups bread flour
½ teaspoon salt
3 tablespoons butter or
  margarine
¼ cup sugar
Pinch of ground nutmeg
3 teaspoons Red Star brand
  active dry yeast for all
  machines
1 egg white, lightly beaten

Place all ingredients except egg white in bread pan, select Dough setting, and press Start.

When dough has risen long enough, the machine will beep. Turn off bread machine, remove bread pan, and turn out dough onto a floured countertop or cutting board.

Grease an 8- or 9-inch pie tin. Gently roll and stretch the dough into a 30-inch rope of even thickness from one end to the other. Starting at one end and working to the other, gently twist the rope. Place one end of the twisted rope of dough in the center of the greased pie tin; carefully coil the rest of the rope around the center, filling the pan. Cover and let rise in warm oven at least 1 hour until doubled. (Hint: To warm oven slightly, turn oven on Warm setting for 2 minutes, then turn it off, and place covered dough in oven to rise. Remove pan from oven to preheat.)

Preheat oven to 325°F. Brush dough with egg white. Bake for 50 to 60 minutes until brown. Remove from oven, cool on rack in pan. When cool, remove from pan, thinly slice, and serve.

MENU SELECTION: DOUGH

♦♦ SQUAW BREAD ♦♦

We always enjoy this sweet whole wheat and rye bread that's often served in restaurants. Try it toasted for a snack.

1½-POUND LOAF	1-POUND LOAF
⅝ cup milk	⅜ cup milk
⅝ cup water (for Welbilt/Dak machines add 2 tablespoons more water)	⅜ cup water (for Welbilt machine add 1 tablespoon more water)
2 tablespoons oil	1½ tablespoons oil
1½ tablespoons honey	1 tablespoon honey
2 tablespoons raisins	1½ tablespoons raisins
2 tablespoons brown sugar	1½ tablespoons brown sugar
1½ cups bread flour	1 cup bread flour
1¼ cups whole wheat flour	¾ cup whole wheat flour
¾ cup rye flour	½ cup rye flour
1 teaspoon salt	1 teaspoon salt
2 teaspoons Red Star brand active dry yeast for all machines	2 teaspoons Red Star brand active dry yeast for all machines

In a blender, liquefy the milk, water, oil, honey, raisins, and brown sugar on high speed. Combine mixture with rest of ingredients in bread pan, select Light Crust setting, and press Start.

After the baking cycle ends, remove bread from pan, place on cake rack, and allow to cool 1 hour before slicing.

CRUST: LIGHT
MENU SELECTION: BAKE (LIGHT)

◆◆ SALLY LUNN ◆◆

Here's an egg bread so sweet it almost tastes like a pound cake. We can picture it on a silver tray with a bowl of strawberries and a pitcher of cream.

1½-POUND LOAF

¼ cup heavy cream
¼ cup water (for Welbilt/Dak machines add 2 tablespoons more water)
3 eggs
3 cups all-purpose flour
1 teaspoon salt
⅓ cup butter or margarine, softened
¼ cup sugar
1½ teaspoons Red Star brand active dry yeast for all machines except 1½-pound Welbilt/Dak machines (use 2 teaspoons yeast)

1-POUND LOAF

⅛ cup heavy cream
⅛ cup water (for Welbilt machine add 1 tablespoon more water)
2 eggs
2 cups all-purpose flour
½ teaspoon salt
¼ cup butter or margarine, softened
3 tablespoons sugar
2 teaspoons Red Star brand active dry yeast for all machines

Place all ingredients in bread pan, select Light Crust setting, and press Start.

After the baking cycle ends, remove bread from pan, place on cake rack, and allow to cool 1 hour before slicing.

CRUST: LIGHT
MENU SELECTION: BAKE (LIGHT)

◆◆ MARGARET'S BUTTERMILK ◆◆ RAISIN BREAD

This bread earns rave reviews from all tasters! It's very moist and tender, and is delicious toasted. Our friend Margaret loved it at first taste. In fact, shortly after that she purchased a bread machine. It *really* is that good. (Note: For the rapid-baking 1-pound Welbilt machine, reduce the butter to 1½ table-spoons and the raisins to ⅓ cup.

1½-POUND LOAF

⅞ cup buttermilk (or 3
  tablespoons dry buttermilk
  powder and ⅞ cup water)
  (for Welbilt/Dak machines add
  2 tablespoons more
  buttermilk)
1 egg
3 cups all-purpose flour
1 teaspoon salt
3 tablespoons sugar
⅓ cup butter or margarine
¼ teaspoon baking soda
⅔ cup raisins
1½ teaspoons Red Star brand
  active dry yeast for all
  machines except 1½-pound
  Welbilt/Dak machines (use 2
  teaspoons yeast)

1-POUND LOAF

⅝ cup buttermilk (or 2
  tablespoons dry buttermilk
  powder and ⅝ cup water)
  (for Welbilt machine add 1
  tablespoon more buttermilk)
1 egg
2 cups bread flour
1 teaspoon salt
2 tablespoons sugar
¼ cup butter or margarine
  (for Welbilt, reduce to 1½
  tablespoons)
¼ teaspoon baking soda
½ cup raisins (for Welbilt,
  reduce to ⅓ cup)
1½ teaspoons Red Star brand
  active dry yeast for all
  machines

Place all ingredients in bread pan, select Light Crust setting, and press Start.

After the baking cycle ends, remove bread from pan, place on cake rack, and allow to cool 1 hour before slicing.

```
CRUST: LIGHT
MENU SELECTION: BAKE (LIGHT)
```

◆◆ RAISIN BREAD ◆◆

On a hot summer's evening, a chilled fruit salad and a slice of this delicate bread are perfect together.

1½-POUND LOAF
1⅛ cups milk (for Welbilt/Dak
   machines add 2 tablespoons
   more milk)
3 cups bread flour
1 teaspoon salt
2 tablespoons butter or
   margarine
3 tablespoons brown sugar
½ cup raisins
2 teaspoons ground cinnamon
Pinch of grated nutmeg
1½ teaspoons Red Star brand
   active dry yeast for all
   machines except 1½-pound
   Welbilt/Dak machines (use 2
   teaspoons yeast)

1-POUND LOAF
⅞ cup milk (for Welbilt machine
   add 1 tablespoon more milk)
2 cups bread flour
1 teaspoon salt
1 tablespoon butter or
   margarine
2 tablespoons brown sugar
⅓ cup raisins
1½ teaspoons ground cinnamon
Pinch of grated nutmeg
1½ teaspoons Red Star brand
   active dry yeast for all
   machines

Place all ingredients in bread pan, select Light Crust setting, and press Start.

After the baking cycle ends, remove bread from pan, place on cake rack, and allow to cool 1 hour before slicing.

CRUST: LIGHT
MENU SELECTION: BAKE (LIGHT)

✦ OATMEAL SPICE BREAD ✦

Our husbands loved this delicious, spicy breakfast bread. Try it toasted and spread with cream cheese. (Note that the 1-pound loaf is baked on the "rapid bake" setting.)

1½-POUND LOAF

1 cup old-fashioned rolled oats
1¼ cups water (for Welbilt/Dak machines add 2 tablespoons more water)
3 cups bread flour
1½ teaspoons salt
3 tablespoons oil
¼ cup brown sugar
½ cup raisins
1 teaspoon ground cinnamon
½ teaspoon grated nutmeg
½ teaspoon ground ginger
¼ teaspoon ground cloves
1½ teaspoons Red Star brand active dry yeast for all machines except 1½-pound Welbilt/Dak machines (use 2 teaspoons yeast)

1-POUND LOAF

½ cup old-fashioned rolled oats
⅞ cup water (for Welbilt machine add 1 tablespoon more water)
2 cups bread flour
1 teaspoon salt
1 tablespoon oil
3 tablespoons brown sugar
¼ cup raisins
¾ teaspoon ground cinnamon
¼ teaspoon grated nutmeg
¼ teaspoon ground ginger
⅛ teaspoon ground cloves
1½ teaspoons Red Star brand active dry yeast for all machines

FOR 1½-POUND LOAF

Place all ingredients in bread pan, select Light Crust setting, and press Start.

After the baking cycle ends, remove bread from pan, place on cake rack, and allow to cool 1 hour before slicing.

```
CRUST: LIGHT
MENU SELECTION: BAKE (LIGHT)
```

FOR 1-POUND LOAF

Place all ingredients in bread pan, select Rapid Bake setting, and press Start.

After the baking cycle ends, remove bread from pan, place on cake rack, and allow to cool 1 hour before slicing.

```
CRUST: REGULAR
MENU SELECTION: RAPID BAKE
```

SPECIALTY BREADS

✦✦ WHOLE WHEAT HAMBURGER ✦✦
AND HOT DOG BUNS

These are definitely five-star hamburger buns. You'll never go back to the store-bought version once you've tried these.

1½-POUND	1-POUND
1 cup water (for Welbilt/Dak machines add 2 tablespoons more water)	⅝ cup water (for Welbilt machine add 1 tablespoon more water)
1 egg	1 egg
2 cups all-purpose flour	1⅓ cups all-purpose flour
1 cup whole wheat flour	⅔ cup whole wheat flour
¾ teaspoon salt	½ teaspoon salt
¼ cup shortening	3 tablespoons shortening
¼ cup sugar	3 tablespoons sugar
3 teaspoons Red Star brand active dry yeast for all machines	3 teaspoons Red Star brand active dry yeast for all machines

Place all ingredients in bread pan, select Dough setting, and press Start.

When dough has risen long enough, the machine will beep. Turn off bread machine, remove bread pan, and turn out dough onto a floured countertop or cutting board. Gently roll and shape the dough into a 12-inch rope.

FOR 1½-POUND

With a sharp knife, divide dough into 8 pieces for hamburger buns or 12 pieces for hot dog buns.

FOR 1-POUND

With a sharp knife, divide dough into 6 pieces for hamburger buns or 8 pieces for hot dog buns.

Grease a baking sheet. Roll pieces of dough into balls and flatten for hamburger buns or shape into 6-inch rolls for hot dog buns. Place on prepared baking sheet. Cover and let rise in warm oven 10 to 15 minutes until almost doubled. (Hint: To warm oven slightly, turn oven on Warm setting for 2 minutes, then turn it off, and place covered dough in oven to rise. Remove sheet from oven to preheat.)

Preheat oven to 400°F. Bake 12 to 15 minutes until golden brown. Remove from oven and cool on racks. When ready to use, split buns in half horizontally. These will keep in a plastic bag in the freezer for 3 to 4 weeks.

1½-pound dough yields 8 hamburger or 12 hot dog buns
1-pound dough yields 6 hamburger or 8 hot dog buns

MENU SELECTION: DOUGH

✦✦ ONION ROLLS ✦✦

The distinctive taste of freshly sautéed onions makes these rolls infinitely better than anything bought in a package. They're dynamite with sliced deli meats, cheese, and mustard.

1½-POUND

Dough

¼ cup butter or margarine
¾ cup minced onion
¾ cup water (for Welbilt/Dak machines add 2 tablespoons more water)
1 egg
3 cups all-purpose flour
1 teaspoon salt
1½ teaspoons sugar
2 tablespoons nonfat dry milk powder
1½ teaspoons Red Star brand active dry yeast for all machines except 1½-pound Welbilt/Dak machines (use 2 teaspoons yeast)

Topping

1 egg
½ teaspoon salt

1-POUND

Dough

3 tablespoons butter or margarine
½ cup minced onion
½ cup water (for Welbilt machine add 1 tablespoon more water)
1 egg
2 cups all-purpose flour
¾ teaspoon salt
1 teaspoon sugar
1½ tablespoons nonfat dry milk powder
1½ teaspoons Red Star brand active dry yeast for all machines

Topping

1 egg
½ teaspoon salt

In a small skillet over medium heat, melt the butter; add onion. Sauté onion about 10 minutes until tender but not browned. Remove pan from heat and allow onion to cool slightly.

FOR 1½-POUND

Reserve ¼ cup of the onion mixture; set aside. Place remaining onion mixture and dough ingredients in bread pan, select Dough setting, and press Start.

When dough has risen long enough, the machine will beep. Turn off bread machine, remove bread pan, and turn out dough onto a floured countertop or cutting board. Gently roll and stretch dough into a 12-inch rope. With a sharp knife, divide dough into 10 pieces.

FOR 1-POUND

Reserve 2 tablespoons of the onion mixture; set aside. Place remaining onion mixture and dough ingredients in bread pan, select Dough setting, and press Start.

When dough has risen long enough, the machine will beep. Turn off bread machine, remove bread pan, and turn out dough onto a floured countertop or cutting board. Gently roll and stretch dough into a 12-inch rope. With a sharp knife, divide dough into 7 pieces.

Grease a large baking sheet. Roll each piece of dough into a ball and then flatten slightly. Place rolls on prepared sheet. In a small bowl, beat together remaining egg and ½ teaspoon salt; brush egg mixture over each roll. Spread approximately 1 teaspoon of reserved onion mixture on each roll. Let rise in warm oven 30 to 45 minutes until doubled. (Hint: To warm oven slightly, turn oven on Warm setting for 2 minutes, then turn it off, and place covered dough in oven to rise. Remove sheet from oven to preheat.)

Preheat oven to 375°F. Bake 20 minutes until rolls are golden and onion is brown, but not burnt. Remove from oven and cool on racks.

1½-pound dough yields 10 rolls
1-pound dough yields 7 rolls

MENU SELECTION: DOUGH

·· SPECIAL ED-IBLE PRETZELS ··

For years, Linda's Special Ed students have made these incredible soft, doughy pretzels once a week for the high school faculty and staff. They've now perfected a touch and technique that far surpasses the skills of those who taught them! So, if your first batches fall short of perfection, we know some very patient kids who would encourage you not to give up hope. For all of us, practice is the key to success.

1½-POUND

1 cup water (for Welbilt/Dak
   machines add 2 tablespoons
   more water)
3 cups all-purpose flour
2 tablespoons oil
1 tablespoon sugar
2 teaspoons Red Star brand
   active dry yeast for all
   machines
10 cups water
2½ tablespoons baking soda
Coarse salt, to taste

1-POUND

¾ cup water (for Welbilt
   machine add 1 tablespoon
   more water)
2 cups all-purpose flour
1½ tablespoons oil
2 teaspoons sugar
2 teaspoons Red Star brand
   active dry yeast for all
   machines
10 cups water
2½ tablespoons baking soda
Coarse salt, to taste

Place first 5 ingedients in bread pan, select Dough setting, and press Start.

When dough has risen long enough, the machine will beep. Turn off bread machine, remove bread pan, and turn out dough onto an oiled countertop or cutting board. Gently roll and stretch dough into a 12-inch rope.

Heavily grease a large baking sheet.

FOR 1½-POUND

With a sharp knife, divide dough into 6 or 7 equal pieces.

FOR 1-POUND

With a sharp knife, divide dough into 4 or 5 equal pieces.

With your hands, roll each piece into a 14-inch rope. Shape into a pretzel by bringing both ends of rope up toward the top and crossing them (forming something that looks like a bunny's head with ears). Twist those "ears" once then bring them toward you to rest on the base of the pretzel (the bunny's "chin"), pressing them down slightly. Set aside on the oiled countertop, cover with a towel, and let rise until amost doubled, about 20 minutes.

Meanwhile, in a 3- or 4-quart stainless steel or enamel (not aluminum) pot, combine the water and the baking soda. Bring to a boil over high heat, then reduce heat to a gentle simmer.

Preheat the oven to 425° F.

Being careful not to deflate the pretzel, gently lift one onto a slotted spatula and lower into the simmering water. After 20 seconds, turn it over in the water. After another 20 seconds, remove from water with slotted spatula. (With a little experience, you can simmer 2 or 3 at a time.) Allow to drain on a clean broiler pan or cake rack. Place pretzels on prepared cookie sheets; sprinkle with coarse salt to taste.

Bake 15 to 20 minutes until golden brown. Remove from oven and immediately remove pretzels from cookie sheet; place on racks to cool. These are best served warm the same day; they do not keep well.

1½-pound dough yields 6 to 7 pretzels
1-pound dough yields 4 to 5 pretzels

| MENU SELECTION: DOUGH |

◆◆ COCKTAIL RYE LOAVES ◆◆

These are soft, flavorful, small loaves—perfect for hors d'oeuvres. Slice thinly, spread with pâté, enjoy.

1½-POUND LOAF
1⅛ cups water (for Welbilt/Dak
    machines add 2 tablespoons
    more water)
2 cups bread flour
1 cup rye flour
1½ teaspoons salt
1 tablespoon shortening
1½ tablespoons brown sugar
1½ teaspoons caraway seeds
2 teaspoons Red Star brand
    active dry yeast for all
    machines
Cornmeal

1-POUND LOAF
⅞ cup water (for Welbilt
    machine add 1 tablespoon
    more water)
1⅓ cups bread flour
⅔ cup rye flour
1 teaspoon salt
2 teaspoons shortening
1 tablespoon brown sugar
1 teaspoon caraway seeds
2 teaspoons Red Star brand
    active dry yeast for all
    machines
Cornmeal

Place all ingredients except cornmeal in bread pan, select Dough setting, and press Start.

When dough has risen long enough, the machine will beep. Turn off bread machine, remove bread pan, and turn out dough onto a floured countertop or cutting board. Shape dough into a log.

Dust a baking sheet with cornmeal.

FOR 1½-POUND LOAF

With a sharp knife, divide dough into 3 pieces.

FOR 1-POUND LOAF

With a sharp knife, divide dough into 2 pieces.

Roll each piece into a 12-inch long, narrow loaf. Place on prepared sheet. Cover and let rise in warm oven 10 minutes. (Hint: To warm oven slightly, turn oven on Warm setting for 2 minutes, then turn it off, and place covered dough in oven to rise. Remove sheet from oven to preheat.)

Preheat oven to 375°F. Bake for 20 to 25 minutes until golden brown. Remove from oven and cool on racks.

1½-pound dough yields 3 loaves
1-pound dough yields 2 loaves

MENU SELECTION: DOUGH

•• SHAREEN'S WHOLE WHEAT •• PITA BREAD

We find ourselves making these whole wheat pitas quite often. Their whole-some goodness, relatively few calories, and ease of preparation make them a pleasant, light alternative to the heavier whole grain breads. Linda's niece Shareen rates these pitas as her all-time favorite. They're so delicious, she likes eating them plain.

1½-POUND	1-POUND
1⅛ cups water (for Welbilt/Dak machines add 2 tablespoons more water)	⅞ cup water (for Welbilt machine add 1 tablespoon more water)
3 cups whole wheat flour	2 cups whole wheat flour
1 teaspoon salt	1 teaspoon salt
1 tablespoon oil	2 teaspoons oil
1½ teaspoons sugar	1 teaspoon sugar
1½ teaspoons Red Star brand active dry yeast for all machines except 1½-pound Welbilt/Dak machines (use 2 teaspoons yeast)	1½ teaspoons Red Star brand active dry yeast for all machines

Place all ingredients in bread pan, select Dough setting, and press Start.

When dough has risen long enough, the machine will beep. Turn off bread machine, remove bread pan, and turn out dough onto a floured countertop or cutting board. Gently roll and stretch dough into a 12-inch rope.

FOR 1½-POUND

With a sharp knife, divide dough into 8 pieces.

FOR 1-POUND

With a sharp knife, divide dough into 6 pieces.

Roll each piece into a smooth ball. With a rolling pin, roll each ball into a 6- to 7-inch circle. Set aside on lightly floured countertop; cover with a towel. Let pitas rise about 30 minutes until slightly puffy.

Position oven rack in middle of oven; preheat to 500°F. Place 2 or 3 pitas on a wire cake rack. Place cake rack directly on oven rack; bake pitas 4 to 5 minutes until puffed and tops begin to brown. Remove from oven and immediately place pitas in a sealed brown paper bag or cover them with a damp kitchen towel until soft. Once the pitas are softened, either cut in half or split open the top edge for half or whole pitas. They can be stored in a plastic bag in the refrigerator for several days or in the freezer for 1 to 2 months.

1½-pound dough yields 8 pitas
1-pound dough yields 6 pitas

MENU SELECTION: DOUGH

·· PEPPY'S PITA BREAD ··

Be sure and peek in the oven while these bake. It's like magic, watching the dough puff up into little balloons! The result is pita bread that far surpasses anything you can buy in the market.

1½-POUND

1⅛ cups water (for Welbilt/Dak machines add 2 tablespoons more water)
3 cups all-purpose flour
1 teaspoon salt
1 tablespoon oil
1½ teaspoons sugar
1½ teaspoons Red Star brand active dry yeast for all machines except 1½-pound Welbilt/Dak machines (use 2 teaspoons yeast)

1-POUND

¾ cup water (for Welbilt machine add 1 tablespoon more water)
2 cups all-purpose flour
1 teaspoon salt
2 teaspoons oil
1 teaspoon sugar
1½ teaspoons Red Star brand active dry yeast for all machines

Place all ingredients in bread pan, select Dough setting, and press Start.

When dough has risen long enough, the machine will beep. Turn off bread machine, remove bread pan, and turn out dough onto a lightly floured countertop or cutting board. Gently roll and stretch dough into a 12-inch rope.

FOR 1½-POUND

With a sharp knife, divide dough into 8 pieces.

FOR 1-POUND

With a sharp knife, divide dough into 6 pieces.

Roll each piece into a smooth ball. With a rolling pin, roll each ball into a 6- to 7-inch circle. Set aside on lightly floured countertop; cover with a towel. Let pitas rise about 30 minutes until slightly puffy.

Position oven rack in middle of oven; preheat to 500°F. Place 2 to 3 pitas on a wire cake rack. Place cake rack directly on oven rack; bake pitas 4 to 5 minutes until puffed and tops begin to brown. Remove from oven and immediately place pitas in a sealed brown paper bag or cover them with a damp kitchen towel until soft. Once the pitas are softened, either cut in half or split open the top edge for half or whole pitas. They can be stored in a plastic bag in the refrigerator for several days or in the freezer for 1 to 2 months.

1½-pound dough yields 8 pitas
1-pound dough yields 6 pitas

MENU SELECTION: DOUGH

Note: Don't give up if they don't all turn out perfectly the first time. With a little practice and patience, you'll soon be a pro! Here are some tips to ensure success:

1. The pitas puff up during baking owing to steam, so avoid using too much flour while rolling them out. Keep the unrolled balls covered to prevent them from drying out.
2. Those that don't puff up perfectly during baking were probably torn or creased in handling. Handle them with care while rolling and transferring from counter to cake rack.
3. Avoid overbaking—they'll turn crisp and brittle. You'll end up with something resembling a tortilla chip rather than pita bread.

CHRISTIN'S OATMEAL •• PITA BREAD

As we experimented with various breads for this chapter, baking pita bread for the first time was probably one of our biggest thrills. We laughed at how they puffed up in the oven; we thought we'd created a true culinary oddity. When they turned out to be as good as, if not better than, any pita bread we'd ever eaten, what an incredible sense of accomplishment we felt! So, if you feel like having some fun in your kitchen, try these chewy oatmeal pita pockets. Invite friends or family to join you; young children, in particular, are quite impressed.

1½-POUND	1-POUND
1 cup old-fashioned rolled oats	½ cup old-fashioned rolled oats
1¼ cups water (for Welbilt/Dak machines add 2 tablespoons more water)	⅞ cup water (for Welbilt machine add 1 tablespoon more water)
3 cups all-purpose flour	2 cups all-purpose flour
1 teaspoon salt	1 teaspoon salt
1½ tablespoons oil	1 tablespoon oil
1½ teaspoons sugar	1 teaspoon sugar
1½ teaspoons Red Star brand active dry yeast for all machines except 1½-pound Welbilt/Dak machines (use 2 teaspoons yeast)	1½ teaspoons Red Star brand active dry yeast for all machines

Place all ingredients in bread pan, select Dough setting, and press Start.

When dough has risen long enough, the machine will beep. Turn off bread machine, remove bread pan, and turn out dough onto a floured countertop or cutting board. Gently roll and stretch dough into a 12-inch rope.

FOR 1½-POUND

With a sharp knife, divide dough into 10 pieces.

FOR 1-POUND

With a sharp knife, divide dough into 7 pieces.

Roll each piece into a smooth ball. With a rolling pin, roll each ball into a 6- to 7-inch circle. Set aside on lightly floured countertop; cover with a towel. Let pitas rise about 30 minutes until slightly puffy.

Position oven rack in middle of oven; preheat oven to 500°F. Place 2 or 3 pitas on a wire cake rack. Place cake rack directly on oven rack; bake pitas 4 to 5 minutes until puffed and tops begin to brown. Remove from oven and immediately place pitas in a sealed brown paper bag or cover them with a damp kitchen towel until soft. Once the pitas are softened, either cut in half or split open the top edge for half or whole pitas. They can be stored in a plastic bag in the refrigerator for several days or in the freezer for 1 to 2 months.

1½-pound dough yields 10 pitas
1-pound dough yields 7 pitas

MENU SELECTION: DOUGH

LAVOSH (ARMENIAN FLATBREAD)

This recipe produces a thin, semicrisp cracker bread that is popular in Eastern European countries. You can soften the cracker by wrapping it in damp dish towels for an hour or so. When it is bendable, spread with a curry mayonnaise and add layers of meat, tomato, cucumber, and lettuce sliced *paper thin*. Roll it up, slice it into 4-inch wide sandwiches, and you have a fabulous and unusual late-night snack for a card party.

1½-POUND	1-POUND
1 cup water (for Welbilt/Dak machines add 2 tablespoons more water)	¾ cup water (for Welbilt machine add 1 tablespoon more water)
3 cups all-purpose flour	2 cups all-purpose flour
1½ teaspoons salt	1 teaspoon salt
¼ cup shortening	3 tablespoons shortening
1 tablespoon sugar	2 teaspoons sugar
1½ teaspoons Red Star brand active dry yeast for all machines except 1½-pound Welbilt/Dak machines (use 2 teaspoons yeast)	1½ teaspoons Red Star brand active dry yeast for all machines
3 tablespoons milk	2 tablespoons milk
Sesame seeds, to taste	Sesame seeds, to taste

Place all ingredients except milk and sesame seeds in bread pan, select Dough setting, and press Start.

When dough has risen long enough, the machine will beep. Turn off bread machine, remove bread pan, and turn out dough onto a lightly floured countertop or cutting board. Shape dough into a log.

Grease 2 baking sheets or pizza pans. Preheat oven to 400°F.

FOR 1½-POUND

With a sharp knife, divide dough into either 4 pieces for large crackers or 10 pieces for small crackers.

FOR 1-POUND

With a sharp knife, divide dough into either 3 pieces for large crackers or 8 pieces for small crackers.

With a rolling pin, roll each piece into a circle that is paper thin. To pick up and move the dough, wrap it around the rolling pin then gently unroll it onto prepared baking sheets or pizza pans. With a fork, prick the surface of each cracker several times. Brush crackers with milk and sprinkle sesame seeds on top.

Bake 10 to 12 minutes until lightly browned. Remove from oven; remove cracker from pan and cool on wire rack. Once crackers have cooled, wrap in foil, and store at room temperature.

1½-pound dough yields 4 large or 10 small crackers
1-pound dough yields 3 large or 8 small crackers

| MENU SELECTION: DOUGH |

•• SOFT BREAD STICKS ••

These thick and chewy breadsticks belong in a tall glass on a checkered tablecloth with a big bowl of homemade pasta and a little Italian music in the background.

1½-POUND

Dough

1 cup water (for Welbilt/Dak
    machines add 2 tablespoons
    more water)
1 egg yolk
3 cups all-purpose flour
2 teaspoons salt
2 tablespoons olive oil
1½ tablespoons sugar
1½ teaspoons Red Star brand
    active dry yeast for all
    machines except 1½-pound
    Welbilt/Dak machines (use 2
    teaspoons yeast)

Topping

1 egg white
1 tablespoon water
Sesame seeds, poppy seeds, or
    coarse salt, to taste (optional)

1-POUND

Dough

¾ cup water (for Welbilt
    machine add 1 tablespoon
    more water)
1 egg yolk
2 cups all-purpose flour
1½ teaspoons salt
1½ tablespoons olive oil
1 tablespoon sugar
1½ teaspoons Red Star brand
    active dry yeast for all
    machines

Topping

1 egg white
1 tablespoon water
Sesame seeds, poppy seeds, or
    coarse salt, to taste (optional)

Place dough ingredients in bread pan, select Dough setting, and press Start.

When dough has risen long enough, the machine will beep. Turn off bread machine, remove bread pan, and turn out dough onto a floured countertop or cutting board. Gently roll and stretch dough into a 20-inch rope.

Grease 2 baking sheets. Preheat oven to 350°F.

FOR 1½-POUND

With a sharp knife, divide dough into 32 pieces. (Hint: First cut the dough into 8 equal pieces, then cut each of those into 4 small pieces.)

FOR 1-POUND

With a sharp knife, divide dough into 24 pieces. (Hint: First cut the dough into 12 equal pieces, then cut each of those in half.)

Roll each piece of dough into an 8-inch stick;* place on prepared sheets. Combine egg white with the water and brush egg mixture over each bread stick. Sprinkle with sesame seeds, poppy seeds, or salt, if desired.

Bake for 20 to 25 minutes. Remove from oven; remove bread sticks from pans and cool on wire racks. Once cool, store at room temperature in plastic bags. They will stay fresh for 3 or 4 days.

1½-pound dough yields 32 bread sticks
1-pound dough yields 24 bread sticks

MENU SELECTION: DOUGH

*For crisper, thinner bread sticks roll dough into 16-inch sticks.

♦♦ TEDDY BEARS ♦♦

These rolls are great sellers at bake sales, cute for parties, and a special treat for young children. Each one has its own personality; it's fun to give them names. You can use any white or whole-grain bread dough.

1½-POUND

Dough

Bread dough of your choice,
such as DeDe's Buttermilk
Bread (page 16)

Topping

1 egg, lightly beaten
18 raisins

1-POUND

Dough

Bread dough of your choice,
such as DeDe's Buttermilk
Bread (page 16)

Topping

1 egg, lightly beaten
12 raisins

Place dough ingredients in bread pan, select Dough setting, and press Start.

When dough has risen long enough, the machine will beep. Turn off bread machine, remove bread pan, and turn out dough onto a floured countertop or cutting board. Shape dough into a log.

FOR 1½-POUND

With a sharp knife, divide dough into 6 pieces.

FOR 1-POUND

With a sharp knife, divide dough into 4 pieces.

Grease a baking sheet. Taking one piece of dough, with a sharp knife, divide it in half. Roll one of the halves into a smooth ball; place on cookie sheet for the bear's body. Divide the other half in half again. Roll one of those pieces into another smooth ball; place on cookie sheet for the bear's head. Divide remaining piece of dough into 6 small pieces. Roll each one into a tiny ball and place on the cookie sheet for the bear's 2 ears, arms, and legs. (You can pinch off a very tiny piece of dough from one of them and roll it into a small nose for the bear's head.) Repeat these steps with the remaining dough.

Brush each bear with egg. Place raisins for eyes and belly button. Let rise slightly in warm oven 10 minutes. (Hint: To warm oven slightly, turn oven on Warm setting for 2 minutes, then turn it off, and place dough in oven to rise. Remove sheet from oven to preheat.)

Preheat oven to 375°F. Bake for 15 minutes until golden brown. Remove from oven; remove bears from pan and cool on wire racks.

1½-pound dough yields 6 bears
1-pound dough yields 4 bears

MENU SELECTION: DOUGH

•• ENGLISH MUFFINS ••

Your friends and family will marvel over your cooking skills when you present a plate of these for their enjoyment. (There's no need to tell them how truly simple they are to bake.) You'll appreciate the humble, fresh taste of these English muffins if you've ever tried some of the packaged varieties.

1½-POUND
¾ cup water (for Welbilt/Dak
   machines add 2 tablespoons
   more water)
1 egg
3 cups bread flour
1 teaspoon salt
3 tablespoons oil
1 tablespoon sugar
1 tablespoon malt vinegar
1½ teaspoons Red Star brand
   active dry yeast for all
   machines except 1½-pound
   Welbilt/Dak machines (use 2
   teaspoons yeast)
Cornmeal

1-POUND
½ cup water (for Welbilt
   machines add 1 tablespoon
   more water)
1 egg
2 cups bread flour
1 teaspoon salt
2 tablespoons oil
2 teaspoons sugar
2 teaspoons malt vinegar
1½ teaspoons Red Star brand
   active dry yeast for all
   machines
Cornmeal

Place all ingredients except cornmeal in bread pan, select Dough setting, and press Start.

When dough has risen long enough, the machine will beep. Turn off bread machine, remove bread pan, and turn out dough onto a floured countertop or cutting board.

With a rolling pin, roll dough out to a ⅜-inch thickness. Using a 3-inch muffin cutter (or a cleaned 8-ounce pineapple can with both the top and bottom removed), cut out muffins. Reroll the scraps one time and cut out 2 or 3 more muffins. Place muffins on a baking sheet sprinkled with cornmeal. Turn the muffins to coat both sides with the cornmeal. Cover with a towel; let rise on countertop until almost doubled, 30 to 60 minutes.

Heat an ungreased griddle or electric frying pan to medium-high (375°F.), then reduce heat to low (275°F.). Very gently, place muffins on griddle and cook for 15 minutes. Increase heat to medium-high again (375°F.), gently turn the muffins, trying not to deflate them; cook for 5 minutes, then reduce heat to low (275°F.) and cook for 10 more minutes.

Remove muffins from griddle and cool on wire racks. Split in half with a fork, toast, and serve with butter. Any leftovers can be frozen in a plastic bag.

1½-pound dough yields 10 to 12 muffins
1-pound dough yields 8 to 9 muffins

MENU SELECTION: DOUGH

** CINNAMON, WHOLE WHEAT, & **
RAISIN ENGLISH MUFFINS

One of these muffins, with its whole-grain nutty flavor, cinnamon-and-raisin sweetness, and full-bodied texture, makes a very satisfying morning meal.

1½-POUND

3 tablespoons miller's bran
½ cup milk
½ cup water (for Welbilt/Dak machines add 2 tablespoons more water)
2 cups whole wheat flour
1 cup bread flour
1 teaspoon salt
2 tablespoons honey
⅓ cup raisins
½ teaspoon baking soda
1 teaspoon ground cinnamon
1½ teaspoons Red Star brand active dry yeast for all machines except 1½-pound Welbilt/Dak machines (use 2 teaspoons yeast)
Cornmeal

1-POUND

2 tablespoons miller's bran
⅜ cup milk
⅜ cup water (for Welbilt machine add 1 tablespoon more water)
1⅓ cups whole wheat flour
⅔ cup bread flour
½ teaspoon salt
1½ tablespoons honey
¼ cup raisins
½ teaspoon baking soda
1 teaspoon ground cinnamon
1½ teaspoons Red Star brand active dry yeast for all machines
Cornmeal

Place all ingredients except cornmeal in bread pan, select Dough setting, and press Start.

When dough has risen long enough, the machine will beep. Turn off bread machine, remove bread pan, and turn out dough onto a floured countertop or cutting board.

With a rolling pin, roll dough out to a ⅜-inch thickness. Using a 3-inch muffin cutter (or a cleaned 6½-ounce tuna can with both the top and bottom removed), cut out muffins. Reroll the scraps one time and cut out 2 or 3 more muffins. Place muffins on a baking sheet sprinkled with cornmeal. Turn the muffins to coat both sides with the cornmeal. Cover with a towel; let rise on countertop until almost doubled, 30 to 60 minutes.

Heat an ungreased griddle or electric frying pan to medium-high (375°F.), then reduce heat to low (275°F.). Very gently, place muffins on griddle and cook for 15 minutes. Increase heat to medium-high again (375°F.), gently turn the muffins, trying not to deflate them; cook for 5 minutes, then reduce heat to low (275°F.) and cook for 10 more minutes.

Remove muffins from griddle and cool on wire racks. Split in half with a fork, toast, and serve with butter. Any leftovers can be frozen in a plastic bag.

1½-pound dough yields 10 to 12 muffins.
1-pound dough yields 8 to 9 muffins.

MENU SELECTION: DOUGH

✦✦ FOCCACIA ✦✦

Foccacia is a flat, rustic Italian herb bread that travels beautifully in a picnic basket along with some sliced cold cuts, an antipasto tray, and a bottle of good Italian red wine. This savory loaf also makes a great appetizer.

1½-POUND LOAF

Dough

- 1 cup water (for Welbilt/Dak machines add 2 tablespoons more water)
- 3 cups all-purpose flour
- 1 teaspoon salt
- 1½ tablespoons olive oil
- 2 teaspoons dried oregano
- 1½ teaspoons Red Star brand active dry yeast for all machines except 1½-pound Welbilt/Dak machines (use 2 teaspoons yeast)

Topping

- 3 tablespoons olive oil
- 1 clove garlic, minced
- ½ cup (2 ounces) freshly grated imported Parmesan cheese
- ¼ cup chopped fresh parsley

1-POUND LOAF

Dough

- ¾ cup water (for Welbilt machine add 1 tablespoon more water)
- 2 cups all-purpose flour
- ½ teaspoon salt
- 1 tablespoon olive oil
- 1 teaspoon dried oregano
- 1½ teaspoons Red Star brand active dry yeast for all machines

Topping

- 2 tablespoons olive oil
- 1 clove garlic, minced
- ⅓ cup (1½ ounces) freshly grated imported Parmesan cheese
- 3 tablespoons chopped fresh parsley

Place dough ingredients in bread pan, select Dough setting, and press Start.

When dough has risen long enough, the machine will beep. Turn off bread machine, remove bread pan, and turn out dough onto a floured countertop or cutting board.

FOR 1½-POUND

Oil a 10 × 15 × 1-inch jelly-roll pan. With your hands, gently stretch and press dough to fit evenly into pan.

FOR 1-POUND

Oil a 12- or 14-inch pizza pan. With your hands, gently stretch and press dough to fit evenly into pan.

Cover and let rise in warm oven 30 to 40 minutes until doubled. (Hint: To warm oven slightly, turn oven on Warm setting for 2 minutes, then turn it off, and place covered dough in oven to rise. Remove pan from oven to preheat.)

Preheat oven to 400°F.

With 2 fingers, poke holes all over the dough. In a medium bowl, combine the oil and garlic; drizzle over top of dough. Sprinkle with cheese and parsley. Bake 25 to 30 minutes until brown. Remove from oven. Cool on wire rack or cut into squares and serve warm. Wrapped in plastic, it will keep fresh at room temperature for 2 to 3 days.

MENU SELECTION: DOUGH

·· SAUSAGE AND PEPPER BREAD ··

Planning on hosting a Super Bowl party? Here's a hearty, savory sandwich loaf to serve at half-time with vegetable soup and a crisp, green salad.

1½-POUND	1-POUND
Dough	**Dough**
Bread dough of your choice, such as Egg Bread (page 17)	*Bread dough of your choice, such as Egg Bread (page 17)*
Filling	**Filling**
1½ pounds hot Italian sausage	*1 pound hot Italian sausage*
4 tablespoons butter or margarine	*3 tablespoons butter or margarine*
1 clove garlic, minced	*1 clove garlic, minced*
1 egg, beaten	*1 egg, beaten*
1 teaspoon dried oregano	*½ teaspoon dried oregano*
1 teaspoon dried basil	*½ teaspoon dried basil*
1½ cups (6 ounces) grated mozzarella cheese	*1 cup (4 ounces) grated mozzarella cheese*
1 cup finely chopped red or green bell pepper	*⅔ cup finely chopped red or green bell pepper*

Place dough ingredients in bread pan, select Dough setting, and press Start.

Meanwhile, remove casings from sausages and discard. In a small skillet over medium heat, brown the sausage, crumbling it as it cooks. When brown, remove from pan; drain well on paper towels; set aside to cool. In a small saucepan, melt butter and stir in garlic; set aside.

When dough has risen long enough, the machine will beep. Turn off bread machine, remove bread pan, and turn out dough onto a floured countertop or cutting board.

FOR 1½-POUND

With a rolling pin, roll dough into a 10 × 15-inch rectangle.

FOR 1-POUND

With a rolling pin, roll the dough into a 9 × 12-inch rectangle.

Grease a 10 × 15 × 1-inch jelly-roll pan. Brush surface of dough with half of the garlic butter. Combine sausage, egg, oregano, basil, cheese, and chopped bell pepper; spread over dough. Starting with long edge, roll up; pinch seam and ends to seal. Place seam side down on prepared pan. Brush entire surface of roll with remaining garlic butter.

Preheat oven to 375°F. Bake for 30 to 40 minutes until brown. Remove from oven and allow to cool for 2 minutes. Slice into 3-inch pieces. Serve warm.

1½-pound dough yields 5 slices
1-pound dough yields 4 slices

MENU SELECTION: DOUGH

✦✦ MAX'S CLOGGING BREAD ✦✦

A good friend brought us this recipe and we adapted it for the bread machine. Now the book just wouldn't be complete without it. Share a bottle of wine and a loaf of this aromatic bread with friends and soon everyone will feel like clogging the taps right off their shoes, just like our friend Max!

1½-POUND LOAF	1-POUND LOAF

Dough

1 cup water (for Welbilt/Dak
   machines add 2 tablespoons
   more water)
3 cups all-purpose flour
1½ teaspoons salt
1 tablespoon sugar
⅓ cup finely chopped onion
2 teaspoons Red Star brand
   active dry yeast for all
   machines

Dough

¾ cup water (for Welbilt
   machine add 1 tablespoon
   more water)
2 cups all-purpose flour
1 teaspoon salt
2 teaspoons sugar
¼ cup finely chopped onion
2 teaspoons Red Star brand
   active dry yeast for all
   machines

Topping

Olive oil
Salt
Dried rosemary

Topping

Olive oil
Salt
Dried rosemary

Place dough ingredients in bread pan, select Dough setting, and press Start.

When dough has risen long enough, the machine will beep. Turn off bread machine, remove bread pan, and turn out dough onto a floured countertop or cutting board.

Oil a baking sheet with olive oil. Preheat oven to 400°F.

Rub some olive oil onto your hands. Place dough on oiled sheet and, with oiled hands, flatten it into a 1-inch-thick circle or oblong shape. Sprinkle with salt and rosemary, to taste. With the edge of a clean ruler or the blunt edge of a long knife, make several deep creases spaced 1 inch apart from one side of the loaf to the other. Cover and let rise in warm oven 30 to 45 minutes until doubled. (Hint: To warm oven slightly, turn oven on Warm setting for 2 minutes, then turn it off, and place covered dough in oven to rise. Remove sheet from oven to preheat.)

Bake for 20 to 25 minutes until golden. Remove from oven and serve warm with butter.

MENU SELECTION: DOUGH

** HAM, BROCCOLI, AND ** CHEESE CALZONE

With a little imagination, you can create endless variations of this basic recipe. The leftovers (if you're lucky enough to have any) can be frozen; they'll come in handy on days when you have to put something on the dinner table in ten minutes.

1½-POUND	1-POUND
Dough	**Dough**
Bread dough of your choice, such as Pizza Dough (page 180)	Bread dough of your choice, such as Pizza Dough (page 180)
Filling	**Filling**
3 cups frozen, chopped broccoli, thawed and drained	2 cups frozen, chopped broccoli, thawed and drained
1½ cups (12 ounces) ricotta cheese	1 cup (8 ounces) ricotta cheese
1½ cups (6 ounces) grated mozzarella cheese	1 cup (4 ounces) grated mozzarella cheese
3 cloves garlic, minced	2 cloves garlic, minced
Pepper to taste	Pepper to taste
9 thin slices ham	6 thin slices ham
Topping	**Topping**
3 tablespoons melted butter or margarine	2 tablespoons melted butter or margarine
1½ cups spaghetti sauce	1 cup spaghetti sauce
Grated fresh Parmesan cheese	Grated fresh Parmesan cheese

Place dough ingredients in bread pan, select Dough setting, and press Start.

When dough has risen long enough, the machine will beep. Turn off bread machine, remove bread pan, and turn out dough onto a floured countertop or cutting board. Shape dough into a log.

FOR 1½-POUND

With a sharp knife, divide dough into 9 pieces.

FOR 1-POUND

With a sharp knife, divide dough into 6 pieces.

Grease a baking sheet. Preheat oven to 400°F.

In a medium bowl, combine broccoli, cheeses, garlic, and pepper; set aside. With a rolling pin, roll each piece of dough into a 6-inch circle. On one half of each circle, place a folded slice of ham; then spread a heaping ½ cup of broccoli mixture on top of the ham. Fold other half of dough over the filling.

Seal well by pressing edges together with the tines of a fork. Brush each calzone with melted butter.

Bake for 30 to 35 minutes until golden brown. Remove from oven. Serve warm with spaghetti sauce and grated Parmesan cheese on the side.

1½-pound dough yields 9 calzone
1-pound dough yields 6 calzone

MENU SELECTION: DOUGH

•• PIZZA DOUGH ••

Now you can have delicious homemade pizza in the wink of an eye! If you prefer a whole wheat pizza dough, substitute whole wheat flour for half the all-purpose flour and use honey instead of sugar in the recipe.

1½-POUND
1 cup water (for Welbilt/Dak
   machines add 2 tablespoons
   more water)
3 cups all-purpose flour
1 teaspoon salt
2 tablespoons olive oil
1 tablespoon sugar
2 teaspoons Red Star brand
   active dry yeast for all
   machines

1-POUND
¾ cup water (for Welbilt
   machine add 1 tablespoon
   more water)
2 cups all-purpose flour
½ teaspoon salt
1½ tablespoons olive oil
2 teaspoons sugar
2 teaspoons Red Star brand
   active dry yeast for all
   machines

Place all ingredients in bread pan, select Dough setting, and press Start.

When dough has risen long enough, the machine will beep. Turn off bread machine, remove bread pan, and turn out dough onto a floured countertop or cutting board. Form dough into a mound and allow it to rest for 10 minutes.

FOR 1½-POUND

Grease one deep-dish pizza pan or two 12-inch pizza pans. With your hands, gently stretch and press dough to fit evenly into pan(s). For the 12-inch pans, pinch dough around the edges to form a small rim. For the deep dish pan, press the dough halfway up the sides of the pan.

FOR 1-POUND

Grease one 14-inch pizza pan. With your hands, gently stretch and press dough to fit evenly into pan. Pinch dough around the edge to form a small rim.

Spread your favorite pizza sauce on top of the dough, then add toppings of your choice, except cheese. Preheat oven to 450°F.

Bake for 15 to 20 minutes. Sprinkle with cheese the last five minutes of baking. When cheese melts, remove from oven, slice into wedges, and serve hot.

1½-pound dough yields 1 deep-dish pizza or 2 thin-crust 12-inch pizzas
1-pound dough yields 1 thin-crust 14-inch pizza

MENU SELECTION: DOUGH

◆◆ CROUTONS ◆◆

Here's a basic recipe for easy-to-make croutons with several variations.

Trim crusts from leftover slices of bread. (White, whole wheat, rye, pumpernickel, and vegetable breads are best; the sweeter fruit breads are not compatible with the seasonings.) Spread each slice with softened butter or margarine; cut into ½-inch cubes. Place on a large baking sheet with a rim. Sprinkle with garlic powder and Italian seasoning, to taste. Bake in a 350° oven for 25 to 30 minutes, turning once with a large spatula. Remove from oven, allow to cool in pan, and store in a covered container in the refrigerator indefinitely.

VARIATIONS
1. Sprinkle with Parmesan cheese before baking.
2. Omit Italian seasoning; substitute dried dill.
3. Substitute diet margarine for the butter.
4. Omit butter and garlic powder. Place a little minced garlic in some olive oil; drizzle over bread cubes before baking. You can also sprinkle bread cubes with Parmesan cheese before baking.
5. Rather than buttering bread cubes and baking them in the oven, melt some butter in a large skillet; add seasonings and bread cubes. Sauté until golden brown. (This method uses a good deal more butter.)

** CHILI BURGERS **

You can make these "burgers" as mild or as spicy as you desire with your choice of cheese. For a mild flavor, choose plain Monterey Jack cheese; for a little more "heat," select a mild green chili pepper cheese; for the brave and daring, try jalapeño pepper cheese.

1½-POUND

Dough

⅜ cup milk
⅜ cup water (for Welbilt/Dak machines add 2 tablespoons more water)
1 egg
3 cups all-purpose flour
1½ teaspoons salt
3 tablespoons shortening
3 tablespoons sugar
2 teaspoons Red Star brand active dry yeast for all machines

Filling

1 pound hamburger
¾ large onion, chopped
2 teaspoons chili powder
½ teaspoon salt
¼ teaspoon pepper
1½ cups (6 ounces) grated Monterey Jack cheese, mild green chili pepper cheese, or jalapeño pepper cheese
2 (15-ounce) cans chili beans, drained
2 tablespoons melted butter or margarine

1-POUND

Dough

¼ cup milk
¼ cup water (for Welbilt machine add 1 tablespoon more water)
1 egg
2 cups all-purpose flour
1 teaspoon salt
2 tablespoons shortening
2 tablespoons sugar
2 teaspoons Red Star brand active dry yeast for all machines

Filling

1 pound hamburger
½ large onion, chopped
1½ teaspoons chili powder
½ teaspoon salt
¼ teaspoon pepper
1 cup (4 ounces) grated Monterey Jack cheese, mild green chili pepper cheese, or jalapeño pepper cheese
1 (15-ounce) can chili beans, drained
2 tablespoons melted butter or margarine

Place dough ingredients in bread pan, insert pan into machine, select Dough setting, and press Start.

Meanwhile, in a medium skillet, cook hamburger and onion over medium heat until hamburger is no longer pink. Drain off all grease. Reduce heat to low, return skillet to heat, and add the chili powder, salt, pepper, cheese, and beans. Stir gently until beans are heated through, about 5 minutes. Remove skillet from heat; set aside.

When dough has risen long enough, the machine will beep. Turn off bread machine, remove bread pan, and turn out dough onto a floured countertop or cutting board. Gently roll and stretch dough into a 12-inch rope.

FOR 1½-POUND

With a sharp knife, divide the dough into 16 pieces.

FOR 1-POUND

With a sharp knife, divide the dough into 12 pieces.

Grease a baking sheet. Preheat oven to 400°F.

With a rolling pin, roll each piece into a 5-inch circle. Place ⅓ cup of filling mixture in the center of each circle. Pull the edges up to meet in the center and pinch dough together well to seal. Place on prepared baking sheet, sealed side down.

Bake 15 to 20 minutes until brown. Remove from oven and brush with melted butter. Serve warm. These freeze well in a plastic bag for up to 3 months. To reheat, place in a 325°F. oven for 30 minutes or microwave on High power for 1½ to 2 minutes.

1½-pound dough yields 16 burgers
1-pound dough yields 12 burgers

MENU SELECTION: DOUGH

♦♦ SUGGESTED USES ♦♦

We have found from experience that some breads are better suited for sandwiches than others, some are more impressive for gift giving, others are great for snacks. We thought it would be helpful to include this list of suggested uses for our breads.

SANDWICH BREADS

Brown Bagger's White Bread
DeDe's Buttermilk Bread
Egg Bread
Linda's Easy Potato Bread
"San Francisco" Sourdough
  French Bread
Basic Whole Wheat Bread
Heavenly Whole Wheat Bread
Madeleine's Neighborly Bread
Shredded Wheat Bread
Lou's Beer Bread
Miller's Bran Bread
Cracked-Wheat Bread
Buttermilk Cracked-Wheat Bread
Lois's Rye Bread
Lorraine's Buttermilk Rye Bread
Michael's Onion Rye
Sauerkraut Rye Bread
Dilly Deli Rye
Black Forest Pumpernickel
Rick's Seven-Grain Bread
Multigrain Buttermilk Bread
Marilyn's Everyday Health
  Bread
Whole Wheat Soda Bread
Olde English Barley Bread
Wheat and Barley Bread
Shayna's Millet Bread
Sunflower Bread
Carrot-Herb Bread
Orange Bread

BREAKFAST BREAD OR TOAST

Midnight-Sun Bread
English Toasting Bread
Heavenly Whole-Wheat Bread

Breakfast Bread, cont'd.
Debbie's Honey Whole-Wheat
  Bread
San Diego Sunshine
Apple-Butter Wheat Bread
Daily Bread
Whole Wheat Sunflower Bread
Miller's Bran Bread
Citrus Rye
Briscoe's Irish Brown Bread
Irish Soda Bread
Sweet Oatmeal Bread
Honey 'n' Oats Bread
Dennis's Blarney-Stone Bread
Buckwheat Bread
Sunny California Bread
Aloha Bread
Sunday Morning Apricot Bread
Johnny Appleseed Bread
Banana Oatmeal Bread
Apple Oatmeal Bread with Raisins
Granola Date Bread
Mixed Fruit Bread
Orange Bread
Eric and Janey's Poppy Seed
  Peach Bread
Buckwheat Biscuits
Squaw Bread
Margaret's Buttermilk Raisin
  Bread
Oatmeal Spice Bread
English Muffins
Cinnamon, Whole-Wheat, and
  Raisin English Muffins
Any sweet rolls or coffee cakes

SNACKING BREAD

Daily Bread
"San Francisco" Sourdough
  French Bread

San Diego Sunshine
Herb Bread
L & L Bakers' Dill Bread
Midnight Sun Bread
Debbie's Honey Whole Wheat
  Bread
Apple-Butter Wheat Bread
Whole Wheat Sunflower Bread
Cheddar Rye Bread
Swedish Limpa Rye Bread
Dilly Deli Rye
Vollkornbrot
Farmhouse Pumpernickel
Russian Black Bread
Zuni Indian Bread
Irish Soda Bread
Sweet Oatmeal Bread
Cheri's Orange Millet Bread
Sunny California Bread
Sunflower Bread
Carrot-Herb Bread
Broccoli-Cheese Bread
Onion Soup Bread
Jalapeño Cheese Bread
Autumn Harvest Bread
Zucchini-Carrot Bread
Zucchini Wheat Bread
Crunchy Munchy Bread
Banana Oatmeal Bread
Marmalade and Oats Bread
Sally Lunn
Special Ed-ible Pretzels
Cocktail Rye Loaves
Pita Breads
Lavosh
Max's Clogging Bread

GIFT BREADS

DeDe's Buttermilk Bread
Irish Potato Bread
L & L Bakers' Dill Bread
"San Francisco" Sourdough
  French Bread
San Diego Sunshine
Whole Wheat Sunflower Bread
Lorraine's Buttermilk Rye Bread
Black Forest Pumpernickel

Zuni Indian Bread
Irish Soda Bread
Dennis's Blarney-Stone Bread
Sunny California Bread
Crunchy Carrot Bread
Elliott and Sara's Red Pepper
  Bread
Jalapeño Cheese Bread
Sunday Morning Apricot Bread
Granola Date Bread
Marmalade and Oats Bread
Peaches and Spice Bread
Sweet Lelani Bread
Butterhorn Rolls
Jim's Cinnamon Rolls
Mini Cinnamon Rolls
Apple Strudel
Orange Bubble Loaf
Portuguese Sweet Bread
Shareen's Whole Wheat Pita
  Bread
Teddy Bears
Croutons

DINNER PARTY BREADS

Authentic French Bread
Tangy Buttermilk Cheese Bread
Herb Bread
L & L Bakers' Dill Bread
Anita's Italian Herb Bread
"San Francisco" Sourdough
  French Bread
Buttermilk Cracked Wheat Bread
Lois's Rye Bread
Vollkornbrot
Morris and Evelyn's Old World
  Pumpernickel
Sunflower Bread
Tomato Bread
Onion Soup Bread
Jalapeño Cheese Bread
I Yam What I Yam Bread
Raisin Bread
Cocktail Rye Loaves
Bread Sticks
Focaccia

STUFFING/ CROUTONS/BREAD CRUMBS

MOST AROMATIC BREAD

ON A DELAYED TIMER

•• INDEX ••